SIMPLIFY
Your
RIDING

SIMPLIFY

Your RIDING

Step-by-Step Techniques to Improve Your Riding Skills

WENDY MURDOCH

Foreword by Sally Swift

CARRIAGE HOUSE PUBLISHING
Middleton, New Hampshire

Dedication

This book is dedicated to Sally Swift for leading the way, and my other two-legged teachers who have appeared in many forms, including student, friend, teacher, and mentor. Also to my four-legged friends, especially Sir Andy Quixote (Andy) for suffering through my learning curves, Have Dun It (Blondie) for her untiring attitude toward work, and Fandango II (Fanny) who was only with me a short time but whose spirit will be with me forever. Thank you for all that you taught me.

First published in 2004 by Carriage House Publishing Company.

Cover and interior design by Eliot House Productions.

Printed in China.

Carriage House Publishing books are available at a discount in bulk quantities for promotional purposes. For details about special sales, contact the publisher.

Carriage House Publishing
223 Silver Street
Middleton, NH 03887
603-755-4596

ISBN 0-9670047-4-8

Library of Congress Cataloging-in-Publication available.

Contents

PART THREE

TIMING

PART FOUR

LENGTHENING

Acknowledgments

 $\mathcal{F}$ IRST, I MUST THANK MY MOM, the source of my talent and interest in writing. Her frequent letters to the editor of my hometown newspaper made me realize the power of expressing one's thoughts on paper and how cathartic that experience can be.

I'd also like to thank Brigitte Newton and Joan Gilchrist, editor of *New Zealand Horse and Pony Magazine*, for printing my first articles back in 1994 to promote my New Zealand clinics.

These articles were reprinted in the TTEAM® newsletter, as well as others I wrote specifically for them. I would like to thank TTEAMNews editor Robyn Hood for her encouragement to keep writing.

I also used writing to learn about other people, including a series of interview articles that were printed in *Dressage & CT* magazine under the editorship of Ivan Bezugloff. His magazine provided horse people with an intellectual/philosophical outlet, which is sorely missed among the equine magazines on the shelf today.

Thanks also to Emily Kilby of *Equus* magazine for helping me sharpen my skills further and teaching me to write more concisely.

A special thanks goes to Emily Kitching. Meeting her at Natural Horse Days, Ermelo, Holland, in 1998 was a significant event in my writing career. Emily was then editor for *The Trail Less Traveled* and she began to run my articles monthly.

After Emily left *The Trail Less Traveled*, they continued to print my work nearly every month, for a total of four years! Thanks to everyone at the *Trail* for providing me with that outlet to reach interested horse people. Over the years, the feedback from *TTLT*'s readership has shown me that there

Emily Kitching and Belieh

is power in the pen. I would like to thank everyone who talked to me, sent me an email, or wrote a letter about how much you liked reading the articles. There were times when I was fed up with writing but your encouragement kept me going.

And now I need to mention Emily Kitching again. She asked me to write for her own publication, *Eclectic Horseman.* Despite my occasional grumblings about long hours on airplanes hooked up to my laptop, trying to meet deadlines, I am happy to have this opportunity to express my thoughts and ideas in print again. I can't thank Emily enough for all of her encouragement and support.

Emily led me to Carriage House Publishing. I would like to thank Cheryl Kimball and Jack Savage for taking on this project. My idea had been to just slap these articles together into a spiral bound notebook. Under their direction, with the addition of more than 150 photographs beyond the ones in the original articles, I am really pleased and excited with the final product.

There are several other people I would like to specifically thank: Linda Tellington-Jones, whose approach to learning had a significant impact on how I teach; Sally Swift for the ground-breaking information she developed when no one acknowledged the role of the rider's body in influencing the horse; Dr. Joyce Harman for her patience and gentle guidance, for her incredible knowledge of holistic medicine and saddle fit, and for being one of the chief photographers for this book; Ann Harman for proofreading many of these articles; Andy Foster for his good humor and incredible skill as a saddle maker; Allie Thurston for her loving friendship, witty sense of humor, and turn of phrase as well as the wealth of knowledge she shared (she gave us all "Power Position"), not to mention the six years of

adventures we had teaching together; Bettina Drummond, friend, mentor, and inspiration to keep going; Bruce Olsen for providing me with both my horses and his knowledge and incredible skill as a horseman; Melanie Alexander-Fuchs for her information on timing the trot transitions and amazing skill as a teacher; all the members of Wilton Pony Club for being the experimental research laboratory for many ideas; and Sue MacNelly for her friendship and encouragement.

I appreciate the cheerful assistance of all those who served as photo models including the people, dogs, horses, and turkey. Thank you to Fran Loftus, Jessica Armstrong, and Andrea Parker for the creation and preparation of the illustrations and David Zemach-Bersin for the loan of Max the skeleton. And, behind the scenes, thanks to Karen Billipp for getting this all into print.

I cannot possibly list everyone who has helped me with the content in this book, although I wish I could remember every specific source; sometimes it just gelled in my head. So to everyone who supported this project: Thank you!

Finally I would like to thank Brad Schneider for his help with selecting the additional photos and loving encouragement to see this project through.

Photo models in order of their appearance:
Emily Kitching, Hila Wever, Debbie Burris, Kevin Hall, "Nigel" the skeleton, Karen Rounds, Squeak, Karen M. Stone, Tiffany Burris, Fran Loftus, Richard Caldwell, "Max" the Skeleton, Nancy Magnusson, Bruce Olsen, Melinda Bower, Patricia Paris, Tara Hadden, Mary Ellen Parsons, Johanna Redmond, Gennie Riley, Allison Thurston, Dutch Gregory Schwartz,

Gunilla Wahlberg, Bobi O'Laughlin, Jeri Hartman, Debie Trimm, Joanne Gaterud, Bettina Drummond, Kristen Carpenter, Bonnie A. Binder.

Photographer credits:
Joyce Harman, Emily Kitching, Wendy Murdoch, Femke Kluivers (Foreword), Chris Cassett (Alignment section opener and page 30.), Ann Harman (Position section opener), Waltenberry (Timing section opener), Sport Horse Studio (Lengthening section opener), Berry Patch Photography (title page photo), Danielle Wargerink, Sally Grassi, Denise Sedgewick, Barry, Genie Stewart Spears.

Foreword

I AM DELIGHTED TO WRITE the introduction to Wendy Murdoch's first book *Simplify Your Riding*, which consists of her articles published over several years. In 1992 Wendy apprenticed with me enabling her to become a Senior Centered Riding® Instructor Level IV. I followed these excellent articles as they came out and found myself concerned as it seemed to me they were too important to be lost in the shuffle that so often happens to magazine articles. This book resolves my concern.

Wendy's work, as you will find here, has been deeply influenced by "Centered Riding." With her innate skill in teaching, her excellent use of words, and logical way of thinking, she has made the description very clear, taking Centered Riding and putting greater finesse on it and greater detail.

In addition to all this is a generous back-up of excellent pictures showing in detail each portion of each movement with clear captions.

Another important plus is that this book is equally clear for both English and Western riders. Up until now, the focus has tended to be for one or the other. It is important to remember that riding of the quality explained in this book is applicable to any type of riding with possible adjustments as needed.

This book gives the serious rider a fine chance to mull over the information in all its facets before putting it into practice on the horse. It will be an important addition to your horse library.

—Sally Swift
Brattleboro, VT 2003

Wendy Murdoch (left) and Sally Swift

Preface

WELCOME TO MY FIRST BOOK *Simplify Your Riding*. This book is a compilation of articles I wrote over the years from 1994 to 2001. Most of these articles have been previously published in magazines. A few are appearing here for the first time. Many of these articles were printed without illustrations or photographs. I have added over 150 new photographs to illustrate the ideas presented.

If you were to search equestrian literature I am sure you would find the information in this book written by someone else somewhere—rarely these days is there something unique or new discovered with horses and riding. However, what is unique is my perspective of the information that I have gathered over many years from a variety of sources.

Some of us learn visually, some by doing, and others by hearing a description. I have tried to "cover all the bases" using a variety of teaching styles and descriptions so that anyone can understand the concepts presented here.

If you have briefly thumbed through the book you might already be wondering about the title *Simplify Your Riding*. In fact you might be thinking that there is nothing simple about the material presented in this book at all! When I called my friend Allie Thurston in a panic trying to think up a title on deadline, she suggested *Simplify Your Riding*. Deadlines being what they are, I thought great, and the title was committed to print. Afterwards I realized that *Simplify Your Riding* might appear to be a bit tongue in cheek.

If you look up "simplify" in the dictionary you will find that one definition is "to make easier, to make less

Wendy and Allie Thurston at Wilton (CT) Pony Club.

complex." That is what I am thinking of here. How can I take a complex idea such as riding and make it more understandable for my students? How can I distill this process into easily digestible bites so that average riders can not only understand intellectually what they are doing but also find the doing itself easy? How can I help the average rider do what good riders do naturally?

In my own experience I found that the instruction I received from some teachers was unclear, illusive, mysterious, and required years of struggle before I could figure out what they were talking about. This was frustrating to me. Although I have ended up devoting my life to figuring it out, not everyone has that much time to devote to this process.

When I am the student I want clear, concise directions so that I can be successful. I also like to ask questions. It bothers me when I ask a question and the instructor goes out of the way to make me look bad rather than either answer my question or just say "I don't know." I think that makes the instructor look bad not me. And I still don't get what I want—an answer!

So that's my goal in my teaching and my writing: to answer all those questions that I have about a topic. I want to take what appears to be difficult and intangible concepts in riding and place them within anyone's grasp. What I am really trying to get down on paper is the fundamentals of riding. The things that work regardless of what style you ride. Then we have a common language, not something determined by a judge or a popular trend.

To do that the ideas have to be understood from a variety of perspectives: what it is you're asking the horse to do, why you want to do something, how you and the horse work together, when it's the best time to ask, and finally how to ask. Without this information you are guessing.

Guessing is kind of like the lottery. You buy a ticket (you get on your horse) and sometimes you hit the lottery for a few bucks, sometimes you hit it really big but most of the time you wind up ripping up your ticket and throwing it away because it is worthless.

I don't like gambling especially when it comes to my horse and me. Somebody is always bound to lose in that game, like I did in 1984 when a horse flipped over on top of me and broke my hip socket. I would much rather spend my time and money on education so that I am not relying on luck to see me through. Because there's one sure bet in riding—gravity. Gravity is going to bring you back down to earth if you don't stay on your horse. Gravity doesn't care how fancy your outfit is, what discipline you ride, or how much you spend on your tack. Gravity is the overarching principle we are all subject to, including the horse.

When you get down to fundamentals like gravity, there is an effective way to ride and an inefficient way to ride. Good riding is efficient—simplified! No extra adjustment is necessary so that the horse and rider can move in any direction at any moment if you are in alignment with gravity.

While I agree that the idea of being in alignment with gravity is a basic principle of riding and I've used the term "simplify," I never said that learning all this was going to be easy! It is challenging, engaging, frustrating, interesting, and fun. And it is going to involve both your brain and your body.

Hopefully you will become so curious and engaged that you stop worrying about the goal. Then you will be in the moment and that's when learning really happens.

I know your horses will appreciate the time you spend on yourself and the level of finesse you develop through these lessons. Good luck and have fun!

INTRODUCTION

Learning How You Learn

EVERYONE LEARNS A LITTLE DIFFERENTLY. SOME PEOPLE LEARN FASTER than others. This doesn't make the person who learns slower less intelligent. It just means that it takes that person a little longer for the information to process and that person may only be able to perform one task at a time. Some people are more analytical or left-brained, while others are more conceptual or right-brained. Understanding how

I use a variety of ways to help my students understand how to ride better. Here I am guiding a student through the process of releasing her hips so that she can let go of tension which restricts her horse from moving freely.

you learn will assist you in getting the most out of a lesson.

I like to teach students using three different modalities: auditory, visual, and kinesthetic (or feel). We all use a combination of these three ways (and other minor ones) to take in information. By targeting the way a student learns, the lesson can be much more productive. If I am not sure how a student learns best, I use a combination of all three modalities. This ensures that students will receive the information in whatever form they need in order to have a clear understanding of the material and be successful.

To determine what your favorite modality is, consider the following. If you are someone who loves to read, can easily understand verbal directions, and quickly picks up foreign languages, then you tend to be an auditory learner. If, on the other hand, you had a hard time in school, were better in sports, need to "feel" something before you know how to do it, and have a hard time when someone gives you a long intellectual explanation, then you may be more

Before mounting I often illustrate a lesson with an unmounted exercise. This helps students understand what they are trying to accomplish when they are in the saddle without having to worry about their horses during the learning process. This not only makes it easier for the students, it also alleviates some of the stress the horses experience during the rider's learning curve.

Teaching the Unbendable Arm exercise.

of a kinesthetic (feeling) learner. Finally, if you can watch something and then go do it, or if you need to have a picture in your head of what you are going to do then you may be a visual type of learner. This is important to know when learning to ride. Rarely does anyone learn in only one modality; however by knowing your preference you can understand why it is best for you.

Riding is mostly a kinesthetic experience. Yet it requires the ability to visualize what you want, like in a dressage test, so that you "see" the line you want to ride. Auditory

My stick figure drawings get the ideas across to the visual learners while verbal descriptions communicate to auditory learners.

I use props such as physioballs to highlight what the rider is doing in the saddle. Balls are objective. Their movement is due to the rider's alignment and weight. They illustrate what the horse has to do in response to the rider in order to stay under the rider. Using ace bandages for reins makes it obvious when the rider is "hand riding" instead of riding from their seat.

I carry a skeleton with me to remind students of their skeletal structure. Here, "Nigel" is resting in semi-supine position.

Sometimes all it takes is a light touch to remind the student of what they need to do to make a change.

skills other than simple voice commands and intonations aren't employed unless you are trying to teach riding to someone else. Hence the reason so many great trainers can't teach what they do—they cannot clearly articulate what it is they are feeling. They will talk about things related to what you feel—"squeeze your horse into a lope"—but

not actually give a clear instruction. The danger is that the interpretation of "squeeze" could be anything from a light touch to a bear hug, depending on the student.

From the perspective of the student, if your teacher loves to use images but you need to hear concise definitions (or the other way around) learning can become quite frustrating. In general, men tend to like specific, analytical directions while women like images and feelings. For example, if I want a man to bring his upper body forward to a vertical position I might tell him to "come forward toward the horse's ears ten degrees" while with most women I would say "float forward toward the clouds." I adapt my teaching style to the person and how that person learns best. This allows the students to be more successful and alleviates my frustration when they don't seem to get it. In the process, I interchange different teaching modalities to help students expand how they learn.

Once you understand how you best learn information (description, image, or feel) you can begin to train your instructors to use your favorite modality in your lessons. They don't even need to know you are doing this! When an instructor tells you to feel something, ask him or her to show you what to do (if you are a visual learner), let you feel what the instructor is doing (kinesthetic learner), or for a specific direction (auditory learner). That way you will get more out of your lesson because you are getting information in a way that you can receive it.

This is not a question of intelligence; it is just an understanding of how you learn. Remember that some of the brightest people never finished high school. Perhaps they just didn't learn in the manner that formal education hands out information!

When learning new information it is sometimes useful to have helpers. Having someone lead your horse gives you a moment to concentrate on yourself.

2

Breathing: The Key to a Deep Seat

BREATHING IS A FACT OF LIFE YET IT NEVER CEASES TO AMAZE ME that teaching this simple concept makes a huge difference to most of my students. Breathing is perhaps the most profound of all Sally Swift's Centered Riding® Basics (Soft Eyes,

Breathing, Centering, and Building Blocks). Granted, each Basic hinges upon the other and it is difficult to breathe well if one is not in a good alignment. However, the amount of misunderstanding I find in terms of good breathing among riders leads me to conclude that

This rider has slumped in the saddle. Notice that her back is rounded and her pelvis is tipped back at the top so that her seat bones are too far under. Her chest has caved. Her ribs cannot expand forward and up with inspiration. While she may be able to fill her back, her abdomen is pulled in so that I could still push her out of the saddle with very little effort.

Now the rider has her pelvis in neutral with her seat bones pointing straight down. Her breathing fills her back and chest. Notice that there is a bend in her hip joints. If I were to push on this student she would remain solid and able to breathe easily.

this is something that is insidious in the general population. We could all benefit from good breathing techniques!

Obviously all of my students breathe well enough to survive or quite frankly, they not only wouldn't get to my lessons, they also just wouldn't be here anymore! It is abdominal breathing with back expansion that I find so rare. When I do find someone who understands breathing, that person has usually either practiced yoga or had singing lessons.

Why is this type of breathing so rare? For both men and women, the concept of good posture in our society is "chest out, shoulders back." This posture will automatically begin to restrict the abdominal breathing process and limit breathing to the upper chest. Other influences on how we breathe

are the messages we receive from our society like "keep your tummy pulled in" and "stick your butt out." Injuries can affect the breathing mechanism, as you may have experienced when having the wind knocked out of you when you fell off a horse. And perhaps as babies we unconsciously learn poor breathing patterns from our parents. In any event, the surprising thing is that if we get out of our own way, the body will automatically breathe well. Then it is a question of consciously developing this process into an everyday unconscious habit. Let me explain what I mean.

When you go to sleep at night, your body automatically begins to breathe deeply. Think about the last time you were feeling really sleepy or observed someone sleeping. Did you notice that the chest seemed to rise

This rider is breathing into her chest. Notice how the back is hollow and her chin is pulled back and in. She is attempting to "sit up straight" but this has caused her breathing to be in the upper part of her chest. Her pelvis is tipped forward and down. It is very easy to push her out of the saddle.

Now she is breathing into her back. Her pelvis is in neutral, with her seat bones pointing straight down. Her chest is no longer pushed out and her entire torso looks more expanded. She is now solid in the saddle. I am unable to push her out of the saddle and it takes no effort for her to resist me. Note that with the improved body position and breathing it becomes apparent that the stirrup bar is hung too far forward for her leg. She has to pull the leather back in order to get her foot underneath her body.

This rider is a combination of the previous two. She has hollowed her lower back and slumped the chest down. She is unable to breathe into her back in this position and is going to be heavy in her hands.

Now this rider has filled out her lower back and is able to breathe into her back. Her chest has come up, therefore she is able to breathe throughout the entire rib cage.

and fall in full breaths involving the entire ribcage and abdominal area, not just the upper chest? This is because breathing is a semi-involuntary function. An involuntary function in the body is your heart beating. You do not need to tell your heart to beat every minute of the day (thank goodness!). Making a fist with your hand is a completely voluntary function—it is under your conscious control. Breathing is something we do not have to think about (like when we are sleeping). However, we can also consciously control our breathing to some degree—like holding our breath when we go under water. The more we practice this skill the longer we are able to hold our breath (like doing an entire jump course without a breath). So we can interrupt the natural involuntary pattern of breathing (full deep breaths) if we consciously restrict the diaphragm or muscles of the abdomen and chest. Conversely, we can develop good breathing patterns if we let the body do its own thing. However, the unconscious habits developed over years are impossible to break unless we consciously become aware of how we breathe, inhibit the incorrect pattern, and allow the natural pattern.

Let's look at how breathing actually occurs first before we start to change things. Breathing is the result of a contraction of a very large muscle, the diaphragm, located underneath the ribs and extending from the front of the body to the back (Fig. 1). The diaphragm separates the chest cavity from the abdominal cavity. It is a dome-shaped muscle with attachments rooted in the lower spinal column. When it contracts correctly, the diaphragm pulls down. This creates a vacuum so that the air rushes into your lungs. When this muscle relaxes, it pushes the air out of your lungs. It is much easier for people to hold their breath on an inhalation (breathing in) than on an exhala-

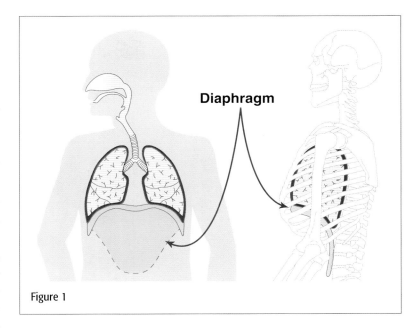

Figure 1

When the rider breathes only in the chest, I can easily push her forward and out of the saddle.

This rider is breathing into the back. I cannot budge her from the saddle, I either wind up moving the horse or the box I am standing on.

tion (breathing out). Typically, if a person or a horse gets a fright they hold their breath on an inhalation—and we all know what

Assisting a student to find the idea of breathing into the lower back.

Pushing on the rider's upper back while he continues to breathe into the lower back. The student gets the feeling of stability created by breathing down even when a force is applied higher up.

So how do we get our bodies to breathe diaphragmatically? The simplest exercise I use to achieve an awareness of breathing with my students is this (performed mounted or unmounted): Place one hand on your abdomen and notice your breathing. Does your hand move in or out with the inhalation? If you are not sure, exaggerate upper chest breathing. You will notice that in upper chest breathing your hand goes in on the inhalation and out on the exhalation. This is the reverse of diaphragmatic breathing. When you are breathing diaphragmatically the hand on your abdomen will move out (like a balloon filling) on the inhalation and in on the exhalation (balloon deflating).

Now let's get your body breathing this way. (Even if you think you already breathe into your abdomen this exercise will help you to consciously breathe better.) Start by blowing all the air out of your lungs—pretend you are blowing out 100 candles. That's right—all of the air. Keep blowing air out without taking a breath in. Then wait, holding the exhalation until your body is really demanding that you inhale. Then allow the body to take a breath. Notice how much deeper that breath was than your normal breathing. Notice that the hand on your abdomen went way in when you blew all the air out of your lungs. Then when you finally inhaled it puffed out like a balloon filling. Repeat this exercise only not so strong this time. Blow all the air out, wait, then breathe in. Again notice the hand moving in on the out-breath and out on the in-breath.

Now see if you can allow more regular-sized breaths to follow the same pattern. You may find that you need to practice this every time you get on your horse for several days before it becomes an unconscious habit. When you are riding, notice if you

happens if we hold our breath when sitting on a frightened horse, right?! The other effect of diaphragmatic breathing is the release of the pelvic area and spine. When the diaphragm functions in this way, the sacrum (the triangular-shaped bone at the base of the spine), which is attached to the pelvis, sinks and there is a lengthening of the muscles of the back.

Helping the rider to bring her upper back forward and up so that the torso is aligned.

tend to inhale and hold your breath before transitions or when your horse tenses. Consciously breathe out deeply before your next transition and allow your inhalations to be full. Notice the difference in your horse.

One of the most obvious things my students notice right away is that their seat becomes more relaxed in the saddle and they feel "heavier" and more secure. Their seat deepens with each full deep breath. The horses also become more relaxed and they will often lower their heads and take a deep sigh of their own. Your center will drop down with each good breath and let you be more relaxed on the horse. Your hip joints will soften because your breathing now allows the sacrum to hang and therefore releases the tension around the hips. This allows your legs to "drape" around the horse and the horse can swing his hind legs under

you more easily. Transitions become smoother when you breathe out and your seat stays in the saddle rather than getting bounced around.

As in all aspects of riding, good habits need to become automatic in order for the rider to be with the horse in movement, including breathing. At first it will seem like you really have to concentrate on your breathing for it to function correctly. Fortunately, we can teach ourselves to breathe better while we are not riding. So practice your good breathing when you are driving the car, washing dishes, talking on the telephone, or in front of the computer. That way, when you get on your horse, you will need to spend less time thinking about breathing because it will be automatic. And remember, "When in doubt, breathe out" and let your body's natural wisdom take over.

Breathing Into Your Back Exercise

1. Lie down on a flat surface with your knees bent. Place something under your head that allows your neck to be comfortable, long and free. Too much under your head and your throat will feel restricted. Not enough under your head and it will be tilting back. Also, place a book on your abdomen.

2. Breathe into your abdomen filling it like a balloon. This will cause the book to rise. In actual fact you can't breathe into your abdomen. However, breathing this way causes the diaphragm to push your guts downward thereby filling your abdomen out. Gently press your back toward the floor.

3. On the exhalation let all the air go out of your lungs. See if you can get the book to go below your starting point, while your back again presses into the floor.

4. Now breathe so that your chest expands when you breathe in.

5. Your abdomen expands as you breathe out.

6. Next see if you can reverse the pattern. Breathe in expanding your abdominal area and out expanding your chest. After doing these chest and abdomen breathing patterns, return to breathing normally. How much flatter is your back to the floor? Is it easier to breathe now?

3

Balance, Timing, and Feel

*I*N MY EXPOSURE TO DEDICATED WESTERN RIDERS, THE WORDS "BAL-

ance, timing, and feel" have become hallmarks in my mind. It

seems that these concepts are the essence of a "good horseman"

and what many Western riders
and trainers seek in order to have
harmony with their horse. I firmly
agree that these are important
keys to good horsemanship. In
fact, these concepts are essential
and admirable goals for everyone
involved with horses whether
their interest lies in English,

Anxiety and/or pain in either the horse or the rider blocks balance, timing, and feel. This horse has gotten his tongue over the bit and the discomfort distracts him. He is no longer listening to the rider. The resulting tension inhibits his ability to balance and respond to the rider's aids.

Western, driving, or simply living with horses. By having "balance, timing, and feel" you can achieve clear and concise communication with the horse without needing to resort to domination, force, and anger.

While I agree that "balance, timing, and feel" are not acquired overnight, it has been my experience as a teacher that by applying more modern concepts of learning, the student can develop these skills that would otherwise take years, if ever, to accomplish. Through employing modern methods, each person can achieve his or her personal best with less frustration and less stress on the horse. (Consider for a moment what it must be like for the horse to deal with the learning curve of the rider. Wouldn't it make sense to use every means possible so that the horse did not have to suffer so much?) The adage "the horse is your teacher" is only useful if you understand *what* the horse is teaching. It is difficult to "let the horse teach you" if you don't know what the lesson is. You could spend countless hours trying and never achieve the desired result. Therefore, by teaching riders how to

acquire balance, timing, and feel, rather than letting them suffer through hours of searching and frustration, both the horses and riders can be more successful.

In order to teach balance, timing, and feel we must start with a basic definition of each. In my experience:

Balance is the ability of the rider to *remain in alignment with gravity* using a minimum amount of muscular effort regardless of what the horse is doing so as not to interfere with the horse. In this sense the rider must carry himself, not hang on the horse. When in correct alignment, the rider uses the torso to sustain self-carriage which allows the arms and legs to hang freely, making them available to apply the aids at the right time. If instead, the rider is out of balance (even slightly), muscular effort is required to prevent the rider from falling off. This shift of weight in the wrong direction causes the horse to move under the unbalanced load rather than where the rider wants the horse to go. Or it causes the horse to stiffen against the unbalanced weight of the rider, thereby going in the opposite direction. Also, the rider's aids lose timing because the muscular contraction involved in staying on inhibits the rider's ability to follow the horse. (To get the idea, carry a small child on your shoulders. Have her shift off to one side then stay quietly in the middle of your back. What happens to your balance?) Once the rider is in self-carriage he will then be able to influence the horse's balance in a positive way by subtle shifts of weight (seat aids), legs, and hands.

I think of *timing* as knowing *when* to use the aids (seat, leg, hand, etc.) *within* the horse's movement (vs. opposing the horse's movement) so that the horse can respond. Incorrectly timed aids do not yield the desired (if any) result because the horse is not capable of physically responding at that moment. Timing also includes the cessation of aids. In other words, if you put your leg on but never take it off then you have lost your timing. So timing includes applying as well as releasing the aid at the right moment. In order to have impeccable timing you must also have balance so that only the appropriate muscular effort for the command is required. If there is an excess amount of movement or tension in the rider's body the signals get muffled and are unclear to the horse, like when you can't tune your radio to a specific station.

Feel is perhaps the most mysterious of these three concepts. Maybe the best way for me to describe it is saying what *isn't* meant by feel. For me, feel is actually the *lack of any tension on the reins and legs*. It is knowing the moment the horse has actually yielded to the aids rather than resisted the aids. It is having the lightest possible communication with the horse, moving toward lightness rather than heaviness on the rein and leg. It is knowing where the horse is going in his mind before he has gone there with his body.

Traditional methods of teaching people how to ride include repetition, exhaustion, negative reinforcement, and domination. These methods have been used by instructors worldwide for centuries. Many of these approaches can be equally hard on the horses and may not necessarily yield students that have balance, timing, and feel.

Riding without stirrups, for instance, is often used with the intention of improving the rider's seat. It may work for some; it may also cause undesirable habits such as gripping with the legs for the rider who is not strong enough in the torso to let her legs hang freely. Longing a rider on a trained horse with a good instructor can be very useful. However, if the instructor is not watchful the rider may still employ her habitual patterns of holding on to stay on the horse—in which case the bad habits are only reinforced. Yelling and screaming at students only drives them further into the undesirable pattern because when stressed we simply react, we don't learn. You can sometimes

get through to a student this way but at what cost to the instructor (frustration), the rider (confusion) and the horse (discomfort)? In the process has the ability to learn feel, timing and balance been inhibited?

Contemporary horse owners—mostly pleasure riders who own horses for a hobby not for their livelihood—don't necessarily have the time, the physical ability, or the resources to employ traditional training techniques. If the learning process is frustrating, demeaning, and painful there is little reason to stay with the sport. This is particularly true of children since there are so many other sports activities available. Therefore, utilizing modern methods of teaching and learning can make the process more enjoyable, satisfying, and educational than traditional methods.

Utilizing modern teaching techniques facilitates the student's learning process and accelerates the time it takes to gain important riding skills. Placing the emphasis on the rider so the horse can respond yields positive reinforcement for the student when the horse does the desired task. In this way the student can develop a repeatable process and the horse can understand what the rider wants more quickly with less stress for everyone.

PART ONE

ALIGNMENT

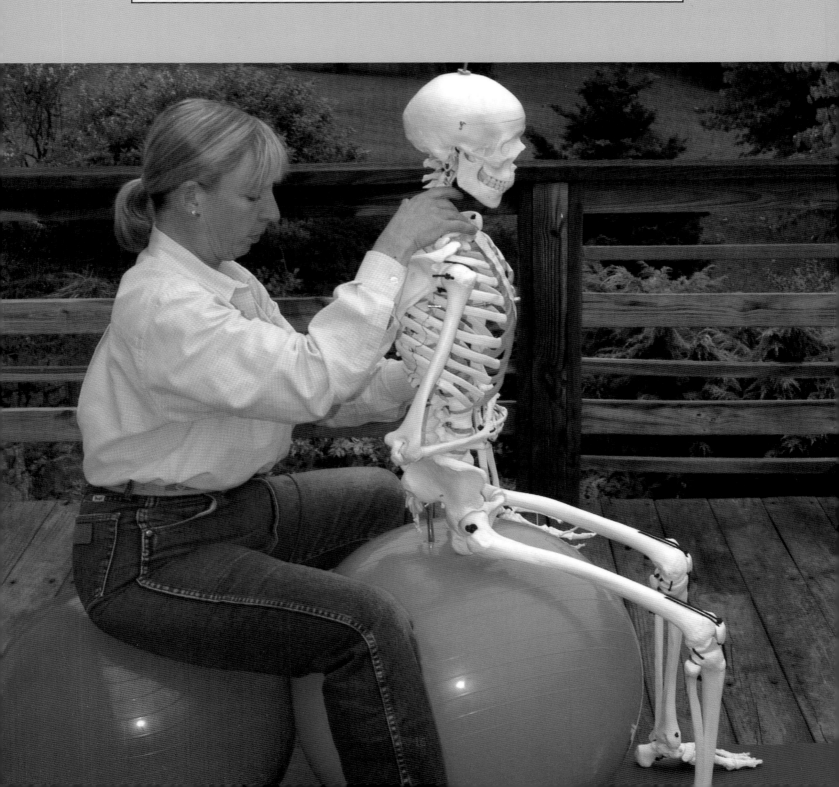

4

Your Head

*T*HE CENTERED RIDING TERM FOR ALIGNMENT IS "BUILDING BLOCKS."
The blocks that Sally Swift refers to are different segments of
your body. Here I will divide Alignment into five segments: the
head will be the first, followed by the shoulders, torso, pelvis, and final-

ly the legs (including the feet). Just
like a child's building blocks, if
your body parts are not stacked
one on top of the other you could
fall down. However, you have an
advantage over wooden blocks.
Your muscles prevent you from
falling down, or off a horse. Your

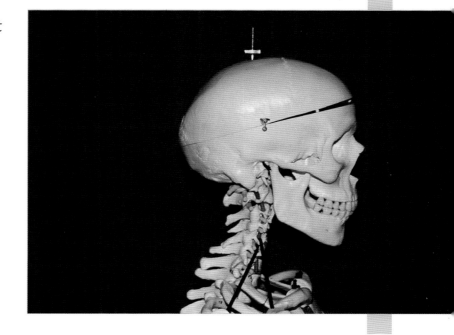

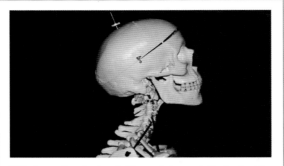

With the neck arched and chin stuck forward, the back of the neck is severely shortened. The spinal processes (the part of the vertebrae that sticks out the back) are pinched. The rod coming out of the skeleton's head is tilted to the back. The neck muscles are going to have to tighten to keep the head from falling.

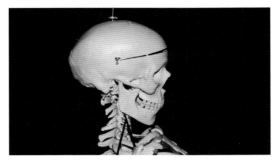

With the chin tucked to the chest, notice that the space between the chin to the sternum is almost gone. The rod coming out of the skeleton's head is tilted forward. The muscles at the front of the chest and neck would be tight, restricting breathing and movement of the head.

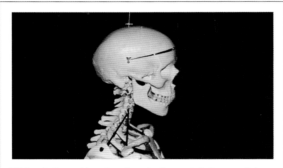

With a balanced head and neck, the neck is long and there is a sense of space between the vertebrae of the neck. When the head and neck are correctly lined up the weight of the head is transmitted down through the skeleton. Therefore the neck muscles are used for moving the head rather than holding it up.

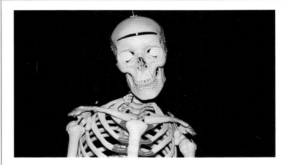

With the head tilted to the side, notice the rod at the top of the head is tilted and the shoulders are also unlevel. Muscles on one side of the neck will be tighter than the other. Again, head movement will be restricted.

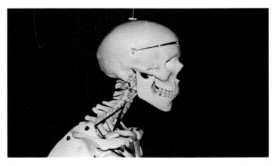

The rod coming out of the top of the skeleton's head is still vertical but the head and neck has moved forward. Notice that the shoulder blades now stick out from the rib cage. Again, the muscles at the back of the neck are going to have to hold the head up, preventing free movement of the head.

muscles unconsciously contract and hold you up. Problems arise because the muscle effort that goes into keeping you from falling off the horse also prevents you from being able to freely follow the horse's motion.

Here is an experiment to illustrate what I mean. Take one hand and shake it. Continue to shake your hand and tighten one finger. Notice what happens to your hand (and your breathing). When you tightened one finger, you tightened your other fingers and your wrist and you limit your

Rider with neck arched.

Rider with chin tucked.

Rider with head balanced.

Rider with head tilted to side.

breathing. Simply tightening one finger affects other parts of your body, making them stiff.

When you are not in alignment, you must contract more muscles to hold yourself on the horse restricting the horse's ability to move underneath you. This gripping generally causes the horse to either go too fast or slow down and stop. Then you have to work even harder just to get the horse to go at all. It is the rare horse indeed that happily keeps going in spite of a rider that is gripping on his back.

When you find your alignment or "stack your blocks," the muscles that were holding you on the horse can let go. Then instead of using grip, you begin to use balance to keep you on the horse.

Rider with head moved horizontally forward.

Actually, the thing that keeps you on the horse is gravity. If there was no gravity, you would just float away. This would make a lot of horses happy and alleviate the problem of sore backs in horses! Since gravity is what keeps you on the horse, you need to stay in alignment with gravity, and then you won't have to work too hard to stay on.

Because gravity is constantly trying to pull you down to earth, if one or more of your blocks is not in alignment with gravity things begin to stiffen and limit your ability to go with the horse's movement. For instance, if your head, which weighs between 10 to 15 pounds, is in front of your shoulders, your neck muscles have to contract. Gently experiment with sticking your chin forward. Feel the strain this puts on your neck when you do this. Notice how having your head forward limits the movement in your shoulders. What will this do to your ability to follow the horse's mouth with your hands?

Just as a point of interest, notice the position of your head and neck when driving your car. Glance at other drivers (being careful to drive safely while you do this) and notice how many people drive with their head poking out in front of their shoulders. This puts a tremendous strain on your neck and can be the cause of headaches.

Now think about your head being poised over your shoulders as if it were floating up like a helium balloon or as if you were a horse and you pricked your ears. Notice how this lengthens the back of your neck and releases your shoulders. How do you think this will affect your horse?

On a relaxed rein experiment by sticking your chin out, tucking it too far in, or having it poised over your shoulders. Notice what the horse does as you change the position of your head. How does this affect the feeling in your seat and the quality of your horse's gaits?

5

Your Shoulders

E NOW KNOW THAT YOUR HEAD NEEDS TO BE BALANCED OVER your shoulders so that your neck does not have to work overtime. You want your shoulders open but not forced back. Many riders complain of rounded shoulders. The cause for this usually originates in the lower back. If the lower back is hollow, and your breathing is not diaphragmatic or deep, then it is next to impossible to widen your shoulders without making them stiff.

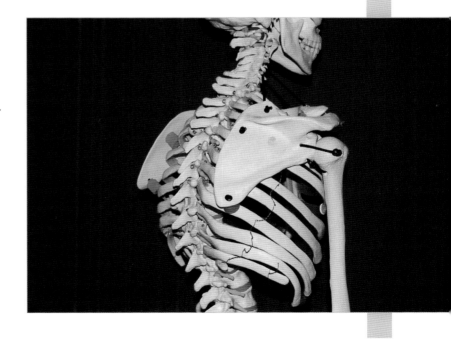

Your shoulder blade (scapula) rests on your rib cage.

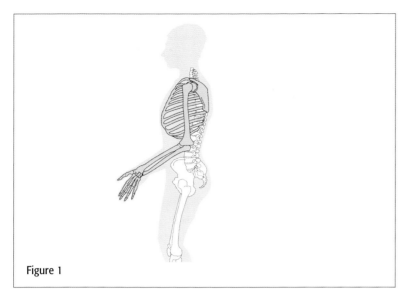

Figure 1

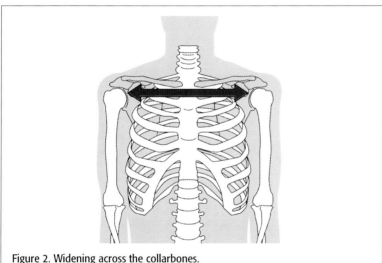

Figure 2. Widening across the collarbones.

The collarbone is part of the shoulder girdle. It attaches to the sternum at the other end. Unlike humans, horses do not have a collarbone so there is not bony attachment of the shoulders to the rib cage.

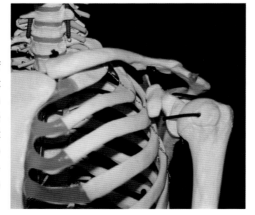

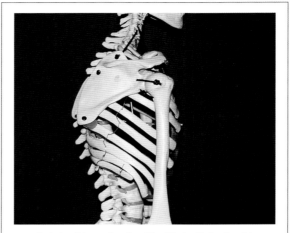

Rounded shoulders. The shoulder blade ("wing") sticks out away from the spine.

The support for your shoulders comes from the pelvis and the muscles of the abdomen underneath the rib cage. As the rib cage expands and lifts, the shoulder girdle (the shoulder blades and collarbones) can rest on top of the rib cage (Fig. 1). As the shoulder girdle settles on top of the rib cage, the head and neck can lengthen and freely float upward. You see already that these different body segments are intimately tied together.

Most riders try to force their shoulders back if they think they are too slumped. The problem with forcing is that you are using more muscles to fix the problem. As these additional muscles fatigue you wind up in a situation where you go from forced to slumped back to forced every time your instructor yells at you. You go right through the middle where it would take the least amount of effort to keep your shoulders wide.

When you are "wide" through the collarbones your shoulder blades will lay flat on the back of the rib cage. You will have more freedom of movement in your arms and your rib cage will move forward and up, in effect lifting your chest. Imagine that you had a smile across your collarbones. What happens to your shoulders? Or think about allowing your shoulders to extend out away from your body. Imagine having a little piece of Velcro® on your elbows so that they stay close to your sides without gripping. Notice what happens to your shoulders. Or broaden your collarbones so that you could draw a straight line across the front of your shoulders (Fig. 2). How does this affect the rest of your alignment? What happens to your horse when you do this? Is it difficult to maintain width across your collarbones when you hold your breath, get frightened when your horse spooks, or concentrate on something else? What happens when you remember to align your shoulders?

Shoulder girdle resting on ribcage.

Rounded shoulders.

Shoulders pulled too far back.

6

Your Torso

*T*HE PART OF YOUR BODY I WILL REFER TO AS THE TORSO IS VERY important for overall balance and stability when riding. The torso is the area of the chest and abdomen. This is where your organs—heart, lungs, diaphragm, back, and intestines—are

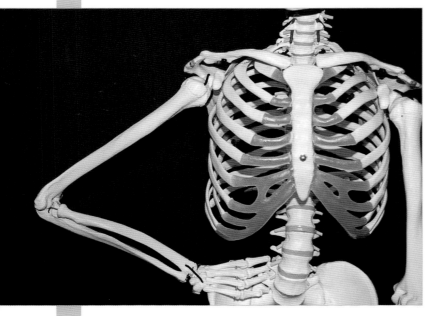

located. There are lots of fascia and muscles that support the weight of your organs when you sit correctly. The key here is to use the right muscles to support your torso so that your arms and legs can hang

The torso is the chest and abdomen. The skeletal components of the torso are the thoracic spine (area below the neck and above the lumbar spine), ribs, and lumbar spine. Front view.

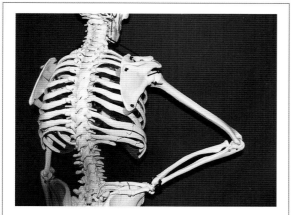

Rear view of torso. (Notice the curvature in the spine causing a collapse on the right side.)

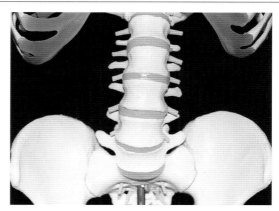

Lumbar spine viewed from the front of the body.

freely, thereby allowing you to have independent hands and legs. To begin, let's consider what "good posture" is. Good posture is proper alignment of your body so your torso supports the weight above it and is supported by the rest of your body below it. Many people think that sitting up straight is good posture. In an attempt to "sit up straight," people pull their shoulders back, stick their sternum (breastbone) out, and pulling their stomach in. Actually, this results in a forced position that is stiff with a hollow back (Fig.1).

This forced "sit-up-straight" position is equivalent to the horse being on his forehand. If you're not sure about this, get down on all fours and see what happens when you stick your chest out. Notice how the sternum drops forward and down, putting most of your weight on your hands (Fig. 2).

After a few minutes of "sitting up straight," muscle fatigue sets in and people go back to their good old "couch potato" slump. Slumping is the opposite of "sit up straight." The rib cage is too far behind the shoulders and the sternum caves in. Slumping is very

Figure 1. Forced "straight."

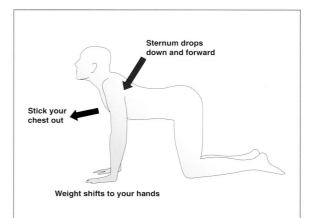

Sternum drops down and forward

Stick your chest out

Weight shifts to your hands

Figure 2. Forced "sitting up straight" on all fours shows the equivalent of a horse "on the forehand."

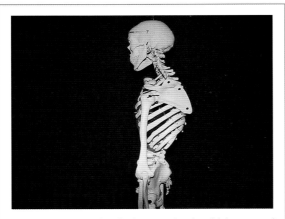

The rib cage is closed at the front. Notice that this has caused the shoulder girdle to round because the rib cage is no longer supporting the shoulders. Also note that a majority of the rib cage is seen behind the upper arm (humerus) indicating the collapse in the chest.

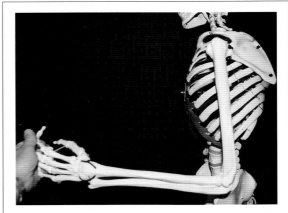

The sternum has lifted and the spine is straighter. Now the shoulder girdle is supported by the rib cage. Notice that you see more of the ribs in front of the humerus than in the previous photo.

uncomfortable for the horse because you are not supporting yourself. It is like having a dead weight on the horse's back.

Good posture places you in a neutral position between slumping and sitting up too straight. In order to remain in this neutral position you have to engage the muscles of the back and abdomen below the sternum to support your rib cage and shoulders. The shoulders need to rest or hang on top of the rib cage. The rib cage is raised (not stuck out) by engaging the muscles underneath it. When you stick your sternum out, you wind up shifting the rib cage too far forward. When you slump, it is too far back. You want to have the rib cage in the middle supporting the shoulder girdle. Therefore, you balance the muscle effort between the abdominal and back muscles to properly support your body in the middle. (This is very similar to what the horse has to do in order to carry your weight correctly.)

In order to help you understand, think about your torso being between the shoulders and pelvis. Now move this area forward and back. Feel that when it is too far back you are beginning to slump. When it is too far forward, you arch your back. Then allow the torso to rest in the middle and feel how there is support for the shoulders and head. Notice a feeling of expansion through the abdominal area just below the ribs. Imagine that you are expanding a balloon in your abdomen. As the balloon expands feel how the ribs move outward and upward. At the same time, notice how you feel wider from front to back. Sit like this on the edge of a chair seat that is level. Notice that you could sit in this position without back support and still be able to breathe easily.

7

Your Pelvis

*B*ELOW THE TORSO IS THE PELVIS. THIS IS A CRITICAL SEGMENT OF
your body because your pelvis comes in contact with the
saddle when you are riding. If the pelvis is not properly
aligned it will cause all the other body parts to shift out of
place.

The pelvis is greatly affected by
your saddle. If the saddle is not
sitting level then your chances of
riding correctly are severely
impaired. With great
effort, you can compen-
sate for an unlevel or

Front view of
the pelvis.

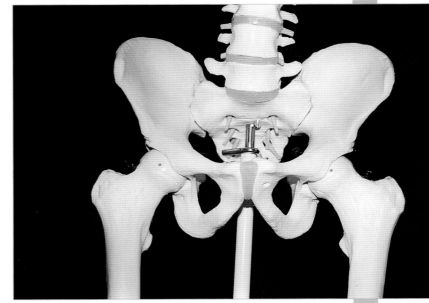

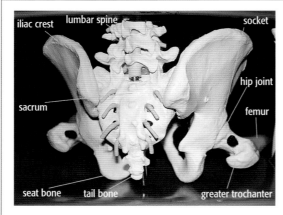
Back view of the pelvis.

unbalanced saddle. However, making a simple adjustment to the saddle can save you hours of frustration and money on lessons by addressing this detail.

To check whether your saddle is level, have your horse stand squarely on a flat surface with the saddle on. From the side, look at the seat of your saddle (Fig. 1). Regardless of the type of saddle, you want the deepest part of the seat to be level. If you were to imagine rolling a marble down the seat of the saddle would it come to rest at the pommel, cantle, or in the middle? Have someone stand on the opposite side of the horse and raise the back of the saddle.

Watch how this changes the location of the deepest part. Repeat, raising the front of the saddle. Remember if you start putting pads underneath your saddle to make it more level that may affect how your saddle fits your horse.

Once the saddle is level, you can start to think about where your pelvis is in relation to the saddle. At the bottom of the pelvis are your seat bones. When sitting in a neutral position you want your seat bones to point straight down through the horse. If they are pointing toward the stifles then there is too much arch in your back. If they are pointing toward the horse's shoulders then your back is too rounded. Tip your upper body forward and back changing the angle of the seat bones in the saddle. Decrease the amount of tipping until you find the midpoint where it feels like your seat bones are pointing straight down. You could imagine that you have little flashlights attached to your seat bones or those cars with the neon green and purple lights underneath them. You want the light to shine down underneath the horse just like the cars (Fig. 2).

The angle of the pelvis will affect how easily your legs can hang down. Your leg bones (femurs) come into the pelvis and fit

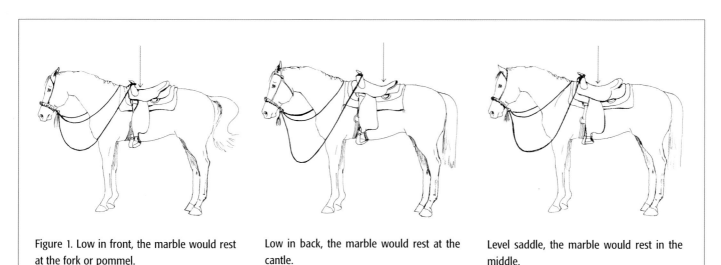

Figure 1. Low in front, the marble would rest at the fork or pommel.

Low in back, the marble would rest at the cantle.

Level saddle, the marble would rest in the middle.

A level saddle allows the rider to sit correctly.

A saddle that is sitting low in front can cause tremendous pain to the horse. Notice in this photo that there is barely one finger's distance between the gullet and the withers. This saddle lifts up in the back, drops down onto the horse's withers, and make it impossible for the rider to sit in balance.

The front of this saddle is higher than the cantle. As a result the deepest part of the seat has moved toward the cantle increasing the distance between where the rider is sitting and the fenders. This will throw the rider into a chair seat.

This well-balanced saddle is level front to back. This will allow the rider to sit with pelvis level in a neutral position.

into the hip socket which is part of the pelvis. If the pelvis is tipped forward or back, instead of level, the muscles around the hip joint will restrict the amount of movement in the joint. By placing your pelvis in a neutral position, these muscles can let go allowing your legs to hang freely.

8

Your Legs and Feet

YOUR LEGS AND FEET PROVIDE THE FOUNDATION FOR ALL THE OTHER parts. If the foundation is shaky or off-center the rest of the building will lean or fall. Therefore your feet need to be underneath you to create a solid foundation. This applies to every equine discipline (although what look is currently "in style" may take us away from what is biomechanically sound). Without your feet underneath you, you will have to use a lot more grip (hands and legs) to override the

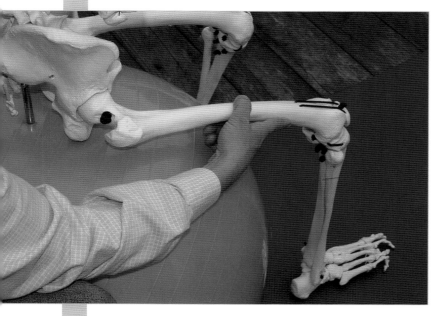

Top down view of the skeleton on the ball showing the hip, knee, ankle, and foot.

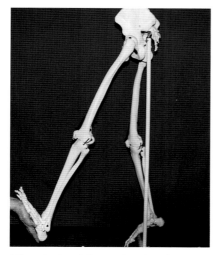

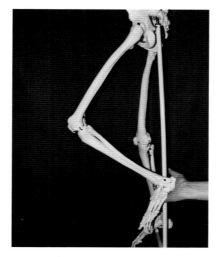

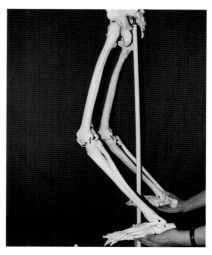

When the foot is jammed against the stirrup, any force applied against the stirrup in this leg position is going to travel up into the hip and lower back instead of being absorbed by the hip, knee, and ankle joints.

The skeleton has a tendency to tip forward with the toes pointing down. There is too much bend in the knee and little support for the rest of the body.

Although the skeleton can't sink in the heel, you can still get a sense of the alignment of the ankle under the hip joint and the stability this creates in the lower body. Notice the bend in the knee.

effects of gravity and the momentum of the horse.

The saddle is going to affect your ability to have your feet underneath you. The stirrup leather (or fender) acts like a pendulum because of the way it attaches to the saddle. If the stirrups or fenders are attached too far forward, the leather will hang in front of your line of balance (as is often the case with dressage or western saddles), your leg will wind up in front of you. This is often called a "chair seat." No matter how much you attempt to pull your leg back under you, the leather is going to keep pulling it forward in order to hang straight down (Fig. 1, left). If it is hung too far back, you will feel like you are being thrown forward and have to grip with your knees. This is a serious problem if you are jumping (Fig. 1, middle). You will always feel like you are being pitched over

Figure 1. The stirrup bar is hung too far forward. In an attempt to be secure the rider has pushed it even further forward but her weight is now too far back.

The stirrup bar is too far back. The leg swings back causing the rider to pinch with the knees. Her weight is too far forward.

The stirrup bar in the correct position. Notice it is vertical and the rider is balanced over her feet.

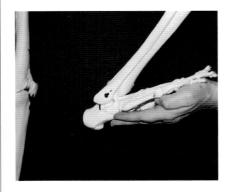

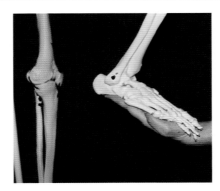

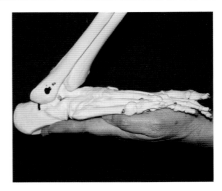

The heel is too deep and the ankle is jammed. The ankle cannot absorb the motion of the horse.

The heel is up. With all the weight on the toe the ankle cannot absorb the horse's motion.

Heel slightly below level with the foot level from side to side. The ankle will be able to absorb the motion of the horse.

the front of the saddle onto the horse's neck at every fence. And no matter how much you keep trying to have your heels down and your leg underneath you, when you jump your lower leg will kick back pitching you forward. A saddle that is sitting too low in front (a tree that is too wide can be the cause of this) can also create this situation,

in which case you need to level the saddle or get one that fits your horse.

Ideally, your saddle fits you and the stirrup leather hangs in the right place for your discipline (jumping or flat work). If, however, you have pushed your heel down too far (yes, you can actually do this!) then it will send your leg out in front of you. Having

Getting out of a chair with your heels jammed down and feet too far forward, feet too far back, or underneath you. When your feet are too far forward you have to throw yourself forward to get over them. When your feet are too far back you feel like you are going to tip forward onto your nose. When your feet are underneath you, you simply stand up without effort.

your heel too deep and your leg out in front of you will cause you to fall into the back of the saddle. It also makes it difficult for you to be in sync with the rhythm of the horse.

The photos on page 32 illustrate a good exercise to see what I mean. Here's how it goes: Sit in a chair with a flat seat and no arms (like a dining room chair). Sit all the way in the back of the chair and put your feet flat on the floor but out in front of you. Attempt to get out of the chair. Notice that you have to throw your body weight over your feet before you can stand up. Then sit back down. Feel how you wind up falling back into the chair. Then sit up on the edge of the chair with your feet tucked too far behind you so that you are on your toes. Stand up again. Be careful, as you will probably be pitched onto your knees. Now sit toward the front of the chair and place your feet flat underneath you. Stand up. Notice that you can easily go up and down, in and out of the chair, with very little effort. Also notice how little time it takes you to go up and down. In this position you will be able to stay with the horse's movement.

Take this same exercise to the saddle (being careful not to slam down onto your horse's back) and find out if you have been riding with your feet too far ahead of you, underneath you, or behind you. Notice that in a rising trot the horse will start to move more freely as you get your feet underneath you. He will be more willing to give you his back if he is not worried about you coming down hard onto him each stride.

PART TWO

POSITION

9

Who Balances Whom?

W HO BALANCES WHOM SEEMS LIKE A SIMPLE QUESTION AT FIRST. Does the rider balance the horse or does the horse balance the rider? On second thought, what seemed obvious begins to get a little less clear. First of all, the answer has a lot to do with the difference between what we *think* is happening between the horse and rider and what is actually happening. But before we get to that let's start at the beginning.

I taught riding to people who came for an educational horseback safari at African Horseback Safaris in Botswana, Africa. What I remember most was watching the African women at camp carry everything on their heads.

What keeps you on the horse in the first place? Newton's discovery with the apple goes a long way to answering this question. Gravity is acting on you and your horse at all times. It is gravity that keeps you sitting on your horse whether he is standing or moving, otherwise you might simply float away. As long as you are straight and in the middle, so that the force of gravity is going in a straight line through you toward the ground, very little muscle effort is required to keep you where you belong. However, should you become a little off-center, no longer lined up straight, you have quite another story. So what happens when things aren't lined up?

Remember seeing all those *National Geographic* photos of African women carrying huge baskets on their heads? Imagine what would happen if the basket was not in the middle of the woman's head. Either the basket would wind up on the ground or she would have to maneuver to stay underneath the basket. How does that relate to riding?

Think of yourself as the basket and the horse as the African woman. If you were to lean off to one side, either you would fall to the ground (if you didn't do anything about it) or the horse would have to maneuver itself to keep you on his back. Don't be surprised; lots of horses do this maneuvering all the time (especially with handicapped riders)! Horses really don't like us to come crashing to the ground. I think it actually scares or at least surprises them when we fall off.

We are humans not baskets, therefore we have another option—if we are leaning we can use our muscles to keep from falling off. However, there are major side effects from this solution that affect both of us. So at first, it seems obvious that the horse balances the rider since we are the one sitting on top and the horse has the job of carrying us. Now let's look at another situation.

Think about the last time you sat on a young horse who was only just under saddle. He wiggled and wobbled all around barely able to hold a straight line. Or perhaps you do dressage and have a wonderful up-and-coming horse who tends occasionally to lose his balance and fall on the forehand.

In these cases the answer to "Who balances whom?" is quite different. The rider, through the influence of the seat and leg, helps the horse establish his balance so that he can carry the added weight of the rider without falling or crashing about. With the dressage horse, the rider not only helps the horse to maintain his balance, she teaches the horse how to change his balance.

Through dressage training, the horse learns to shift his weight up and back towards the hindquarters, which lightens the front end and allows the horse to perform spectacular movements such as canter pirouettes. From this point of view it would seem that it is the rider who balances the horse.

In fact, both of these situations are occurring all the time; the horse balances the rider and the rider balances the horse. Depending upon the ability of each, the amount the rider or horse contributes to the overall balance constantly changes. A well-trained horse is an ideal horse for the beginner because he will develop all the correct feelings of balance within the student right from the start. A top rider is the best for a young horse for all the same reasons. The experienced rider can maintain his or her own balance as the horse learns how to carry himself.

The ideal situation (one of the ultimate goals in dressage) between a horse and rider is that they each are able to maintain their own "self-carriage" at all times. We often think of horses in "self-carriage" independently maintaining balance without the influence of the rider. It is not something we often refer to in the rider; however in order for the horse to achieve self-carriage, the rider must be able to support himself without having to hang onto the horse's mouth with the reins or clamp on with his legs. So what happens to horses and riders that are somewhere between these two extremes?

We must go back to what happens when gravity is acting on a rider that is not sitting straight on the horse's back. When gravity acts on a body that is off-center, the action of the force will be more in one place than the other (Figs. 1 and 2).

In order for the rider to stay on, voluntary muscles must be used. The contraction of these muscles for the purpose of staying on causes stiffness in the rider. The stiffness then causes the rider to lose his balance even more, because he will not be able to

fluidly follow the horse's movement causing the horse to stiffen in the corresponding parts of his body. Overall it will become harder for the rider to stay in balance and harder for the horse to move well. The goal then is for the rider to find pure balance in the saddle without having to grip or tighten, at all gaits, so that the horse no longer has to adjust himself like the African woman carrying the unbalanced basket.

How can riders determine if they are partly the cause of their horses' stiffness and training difficulties? Look at photos of you riding your horse or better yet have someone video you. Take pictures of you moving on a straight line from the front and rear as well as side-on. Ask yourself: "Am I collapsing through the rib cage, am I leaning too far forward, is my back hollow and stiff, or have I rounded my shoulders?"

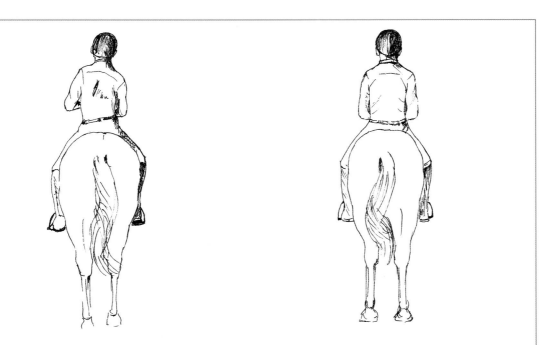

Figure 1. Rear view of rider: collapsing to the right (left) and sitting in balance (right). Notice the difference in the shoulders and hips. The rider on the left will have difficulties keeping the horse from falling in to the right and will be stiff to the left. This rider will constantly be losing one stirrup. The rider on the right will be able to go well on either rein and will have no trouble keeping his feet in the stirrups. This rider's body will be more supple and able to follow the horse's movement.

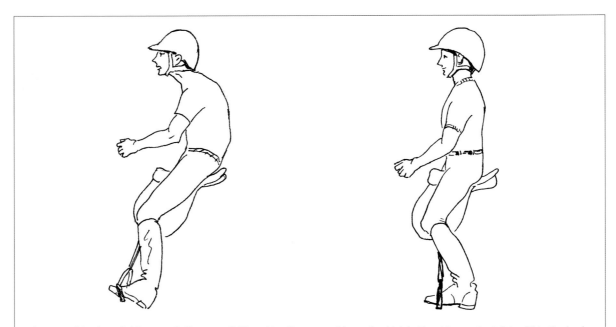

Figure 2. Side view of rider out of alignment (left) and in alignment with gravity (right). The rider on the left is stiff in the back, neck, seat, and leg. His horse will have difficulty using his back and will generally be heavy on the forehand. The rider on the right is central in the saddle with gravity acting through the center of his body. This rider will not interfere with the horse's balance and will be free in his hips, seat, and legs to correctly time the use of his aids.

Look at photos of really top riders such as Arthur Kottas-Heldenberg and notice that if you were to draw a line down through the middle of him or across his shoulders, the lines are straight and square. Next time you ride, imagine that you are sitting as straight as these riders do and see what happens.

Another test is to see if you can walk, trot, and canter without using your reins for balance. If not, begin to explore where you tighten at the walk. Allow yourself some time for self-exploration. Ask yourself: "Are my hip joints 'greasy' and free, can my seat bones follow the movement of the horse's back at the walk, if I let go of the reins are my shoulders hanging freely and swinging with the movement, or do they feel tight?"

Then notice what happens to your horse as you begin to become more aware of the movement in your body. Ask yourself if your horse is tight in the same places you are and notice what happens as you relax and loosen up those places.

Once you find pure balance in the saddle, all the effort that went into keeping you on the horse can now go into improving your performance rather than just keeping you on board. Your ability to move and follow will make everything easier and more enjoyable. Most importantly, you will make your horse's job of carrying you a lot easier and he will thank you for it by becoming a more willing, cooperative partner.

10

Rebalance Your Riding Image

FTER THE LAST CHAPTER YOU MAY HAVE DRAGGED OUT YOUR cameras and your friends and convinced them that they need to take still photos or videos of you. Now what?

TAKE A LOOK AT WHAT YOU HAVE

First, let's take a look at what you have. Grab a ruler and draw a straight line down through the middle of your body from head to seat (photos taken from the back are best for this). Continue the line down through the saddle and

Do you look like a turkey on your horse?

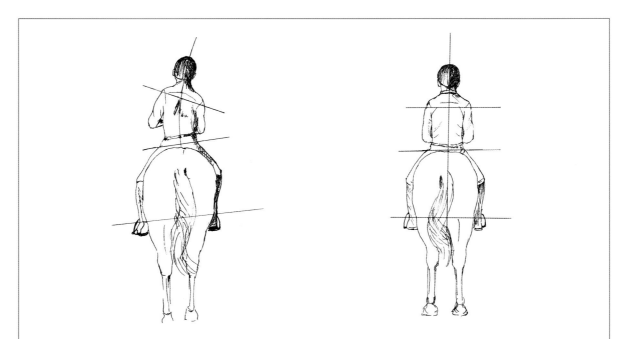

Figure 1. In these rear views, horizontal lines have been drawn through the riders' shoulders, hips, and feet. A vertical line has been drawn through the middle of the body from head to seat. The lines drawn through the rider on the left show a collapse on the right side of the rib cage, resulting in a dropped right shoulder and raised right hip. Notice that the right leg is drawn up with the hip and the head is tipped to the right. The lines drawn through the rider on the right are parallel. This rider is sitting straight and square on his horse.

horse to see if your saddle is sitting straight or off to one side of the horse's back.

If you are doing this from a video, run the tape, then put it on still. Hopefully, you have a clear picture. Take tracing paper and draw an outline of your body. Then draw in the straight lines as above. Or, you could simply hold the ruler up to the TV screen.

Draw horizontal lines through your shoulders and hips (Fig. 1). The crease in your leg right at the top of the thigh that will give you good indication of where the hip joint is. If you have a photo from the side, draw a vertical line through your hip perpendicular to the ground. Now look and see what you've got.

If the lines running through your shoulders and hips are parallel when viewed from the back, congratulations! You are one of the rare few who are straight. I have yet to see anyone who is perfectly symmetrical. Why? Because as we go through life our bodies are affected by the things we do. Very often we engage in activities that develop our muscles asymmetrically or we injure ourselves and develop compensations.

Go back to the side-on shot. Does the line run through your ear, shoulder, hip, and ankle (Fig. 2)? Check to see if your stirrup leather is straight. You may have pulled your stirrup back in an attempt to get your leg underneath you. Or perhaps you are jamming your heels down and forcing the leather forward and out of alignment (see Chapter 9).

Depending upon the type of saddle and where the stirrup bar has been placed, when the leather is straight your leg may not be underneath you. If it is a jumping saddle this

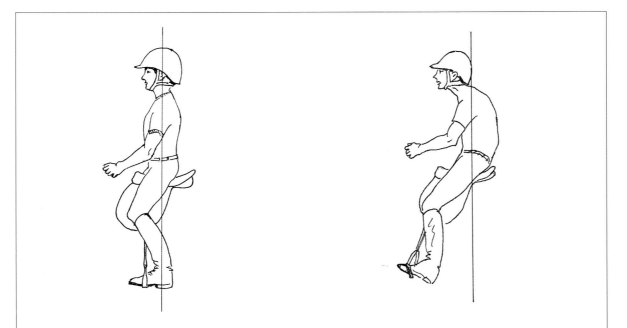

Figure 2. Vertical lines have been drawn through the hip joint of these riders viewed from the side. In the figure on the left the line travels through the rider in the classical alignment of ear, shoulder, hip, and ankle. Notice that the stirrup leather is straight and parallel to the line through the rider. The rider on the right is sitting in a slumped position. The line through the rider's hip passes behind the ear, in front of the shoulder, through the hip, and well behind the ankle. Notice that the leather has been forced forward by excessive pressure into the rider's heel and the chin is jutting forward in order for the head to be over the feet. This rider is locked in the hip joints and will have to use the reins to maintain his balance.

could be correct. For jumping, the stirrup bar should be more forward because your leathers are shorter and you are out of your saddle going over a jump.

If it is a dressage or Western saddle, your leg should be able to hang straight down underneath you without having to fight with your stirrups. If the leather is angled back when your ankle is under your hip, then the stirrup bar is placed too far forward on the tree.

You can attempt to pull your feet back every time you think about them; however, the leather will continually pull your feet forward and every time you shift your awareness to something else, your leg will creep out in front of you again.

The best solution to this problem is to get a different saddle. If this isn't practical, you can try putting a spacer on the bar (although this isn't safe for jumping) or use an Equiband® (see my website for more on these) to help train your position.

After looking at the stirrup leather, take a look at your back. Is it hollow or round? Are your shoulders pulled back in tension, rounded forward, or comfortably wide and open? Is your head over your shoulders? Or are you leading with your chin (this position will cause tension down your entire back and affect your breathing).

MAKING THINGS RIGHT
Well, by now I am sure you have a real good idea what's wrong. So, how do we go about making things right? Here are two exercises you can do to help straighten yourself out, but first, try the following test.

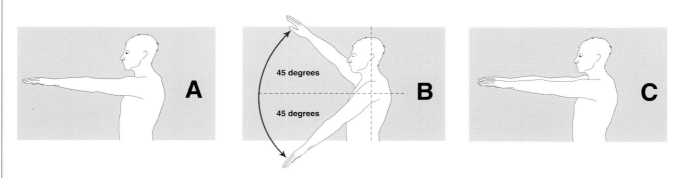

Figure 3. Exploring our perception of reality (side view). a) Hold both arms straight out in front of you. b) With your eyes closed, raise one arm up 45 degrees and the other arm down 45 degrees. Hold your arms in this position, keeping your eyes closed for at least 45 seconds. c) Bring your arms level in front of you, then open your eyes. Notice if your arms are at the same height or if one is slightly higher or lower than the other.

You will need to read the instructions before you begin because you have to do the exercise with your eyes closed (Fig. 3).

An Exercise to Explore Your Perception

Close your eyes. Hold both arms straight out in front of you. Raise one arm up to a 45-degree angle and the other arm down at a 45-degree angle from your original position. Wait 45 seconds.

With your eyes still closed, bring both arms to level in front of you again. Open your eyes.

Are your arms actually even with each other like you thought they were, or is one arm slightly higher than the other? If one arm is higher than the other you are in the majority.

The point is that our perception of our bodies is not always accurate. We may think that we are doing something to the extreme, yet we have barely changed. Consider the last time your instructor told you to get your leg back underneath you. You thought it couldn't go any further back but the instructor wasn't satisfied. From her perspective, the leg was still way too far forward; from yours, it was already back.

When you begin to make changes in your position, your body may scream at you. You may feel like you are falling forward or back or off to one side. Take another photo or video and check it out. Let an objective observer, either yourself from photos or someone on the ground, help you decide if your position is more aligned.

Collapsing Through the Rib Cage

If you are collapsing through the rib cage, dropping one shoulder, or sitting unevenly on your seat bones, play with the following exercise.

Using the hand on the side that is collapsed, place the thumb side of your hand, fingers pointing straight up, on your sternum (breastbone). Raise your hand up over your head so that your elbow is alongside of your ear, your arm straight with your thumb pointing toward the back of the horse.

Feel the opening of the rib cage on the side that was previously collapsed. Notice that the weight will go diagonally through your body and allow the seat bone on the opposite side to sink down into the saddle or laterally so that the seat bone on the same side as your raised arm goes down.

Ride at walk, trot, and canter with your arm over your head. If you feel your elbow dropping, then something has tightened

A simple correction for collapsing one side of your torso is to extend your arm over your head. As long as there is no discomfort in your shoulder it is important to extend the arm with the elbow straight with the fingers extended towards the sky and your thumb pointing towards the horse's tail.

Here the elbow is bent. Notice the tightness in the rider's neck and shoulders. The rib cage has not opened and the shoulder is still restricted. In this position there is little to no benefit from extending the arm overhead.

(most likely your hips) and you are starting to contract on that side of your body. See if you can let your fingers grow toward the sky. (Rest your arm if you need to!)

Notice whether your horse moves more freely and straight, instead of cutting the corners of the arena. Experiment raising and lowering your arm.

Let your arm down and keep the image and feeling of it in the air in your mind. If you need to, put your arm up again and remind yourself of the feeling.

Experiment with putting the other arm in the air. Generally, people feel more comfortable putting up the arm that does not correct the collapse because it feels more familiar. If the rider has a curvature of the spine the arm on the opposite side to the collapsing ribs may need to be in the air. Have someone on the ground watch you from the back or take more photos or videos and see which arm works better for you.

Getting into Alignment

The next exercise will improve your position in terms of the classical alignment of a straight line through your ear, shoulder, hip, and ankle (side view).

Take your feet out of the stirrups. Imagine that your seat bones have two tiny flashlights attached to them. Notice whether the light from the flashlights are pointing toward the horse's nose, tail, or straight down through the saddle to the ground.

From your seat bones, teeter-totter forward and back until it feels like the lights point straight towards the ground. Exaggerate the teeter-totter at first, going through the

Figure 4. Think of flashlights on your seat bones pointing toward the rear of the horse (left), straight down (middle), or toward the front of the horse (right). Notice that the stirrup leather is pushed out of alignment in the two end figures and that the pelvis is tipped down and forward and back and up in the left and right figures respectively. This will cause tightness in the hip joints and make it difficult to ride without unnecessary tension in the body.

mid-point well forward and back, then gradually decrease the size of the oscillations.

Once you have found the place where the light shines straight down, place one hand on your lower back and notice if it is hollow, rounded, or full. Gradually lengthen up through your back and out the top of your head. Be careful to keep your back full as you lengthen. Only grow up as long as your back remains full. If your back starts to hollow, stop and sink down just a little. You may feel slumped at this height. That is not unusual especially if you are the type of rider who has been stiff in the back.

Notice your breathing. You want to breathe all the way down to your toes and let your whole body expand with each inhalation.

Allow your collarbones to grow wide across the front of your body. Be careful not to "sit up straight" to do this as this is often the cause of stiffness in the back. Avoid pulling the shoulders back with the muscles of the shoulder blades. Instead, think of the release

coming from the collarbones themselves.

Let your head float up like a helium balloon and allow your body to hang from the string.

Finally, place your feet back in the stirrups without stiffening the ankles, knees, or hips. Only the weight of your leg should rest in the stirrups. Imagine your feet growing down to the ground. Let your heels sink down toward your horse's hind feet.

As your horse begins to move continue to notice if your feet feel like they could touch the ground, whether or not your seat bones continue to shine a light directly underneath you, and if your head continues to float over the top of you.

Have someone take another photo and see what kind of changes have occurred.

This exercise will help you to find a classical alignment for dressage, Western, and pleasure riding. For jumping position, shorten your stirrups, then simply come up out of the saddle by angling your upper body forward and let your buttocks go back, keeping your back flat and your weight over your feet (Fig. 5). This will allow your hip, knee, and ankle to continue functioning as shock absorbers instead of being crammed into a rigid position.

WHERE THIS LEAVES YOU NOW

Ideally, someone on the ground could point out your alignment and you would have the awareness to alter your position. However, many riders ride on their own and sometimes it takes some encouraging hands to help the body to find the new place. If you find you're getting resistant to change, take a moment and breathe into the tightness. Let the movement of the horse loosen the stiff spots. Give yourself permission to be stuck for a moment, then notice if anything has changed. Start becoming aware of your habitual patterns when you are off the horse and notice if you continue them when you ride. Most importantly, let your horse tell you if you are making progress. Often, the horse is far more tolerant of our inabilities than we realize and he is happy to tell us when we have let go of tension thereby making his job easier.

Figure 5. In jumping position, the rider maintains her balance over her feet. The angles of the hip, knee, and ankle have closed. The rider's weight sinks into her heels because the ankle is supple. Notice that the stirrup leather is vertical and that the hips have moved back as the upper body inclines forward maintaining the rider's weight over her feet.

11

How Secure Is Your Seat?

ONE OF THE MOST IMPORTANT ATTRIBUTES TO ANY GOOD RIDER IS A
secure, independent seat. This good seat needs to stay "glued"
to the saddle should the horse pull any unexpected moves such
as shying, bucking, or fast turns. A secure seat is particularly impor-

tant when riding young horses. The
young horse lacks experience which
often leads to unexpected rapid
movements. Lurking critters like
wheelbarrows or a cat in the bushes
are sure to get a reaction. The last
thing a young horse needs is for you
to become a projectile missile.

I am sure that a flying Karamozov rider is far more upsetting to the horse than we can imagine. Just think about it for a second. The horse has entrusted himself to you and yet you abandon him in his moment of need! Or worse yet, what he needs is reassurance but what he gets is the rider pounding on his back every time he jumps a little. All of a sudden the scary thing the horse spooked at in the first place isn't his only problem. Now that scary thing has somehow mysteriously gotten on his back and is attacking! How did this happen? What should the horse do about it? If I were a horse, I would try to remove it as quickly as possible, wouldn't you?

There are a number of reasons why the rider with the less educated seat is more likely to come to a bad end than the experienced rider. First, the experienced rider can evaluate the situation and either prevent or defuse the problem before it ever gets out of control. Second, the experienced rider generally has an independent seat that is more capable of riding out a buck or sideways spook by remaining relaxed and therefore causing less distress to the horse. Third, since there is less pounding on the horse's back, the horse is likely to decrease the degree of reaction because the rider is not contributing to the horse's pain and fear.

In order to achieve an independent seat the rider needs to be able to sit deep in the saddle with a minimum of muscle effort. When the rider sits in alignment with gravity the skeleton supports the body rather than bracing shoulders or legs against the tack. Once the rider is in skeletal support the postural muscles (the ones designed to hold us upright) take on their proper role. The postural muscles include the abdominal and back muscles.

Watch toddlers just learning to get around. They demonstrate exquisite use of their pos-

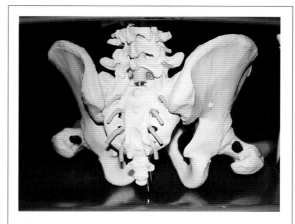

The back side of pelvis and sacrum.

Postural muscles are required to balance the head while sitting up.

tural muscles so that they can balance their head over their feet. Unfortunately this is something we lose as we grow and develop voluntary muscle strength unless we practice good posture (who does that?). As we mature we learn fine motor control and allow the furniture and our joints to hold us instead of continuing to maintain our postural muscles. In order to ride well we need to reestablish our postural muscle support whose primary role is to stabilize the torso and head so that our limbs can hang freely. In order for the postural support mechanism to function properly the pelvis needs to be in a neutral position.

The different positions in the pelvis have a direct effect on the rider's overall security. With the rider's seat bones pointing straight down her weight is over her seat (left). With her seat bones pointed toward the back, her back is arched (middle). With her seat bones pointing toward the front, her back is rounded (right).

To sit with the pelvis in a neutral position, the seat bones (the part of the pelvis that is the equivalent to the point of the buttocks on the horse) need to point straight down. Find your seat bones by sitting on your hand on a fairly hard surface. Be careful because you may be surprised at how uncomfortable this can be to your hand. While sitting on your hand change the angle of your pelvis and feel how you can roll on and off your seat bones. As you round your back notice that you have rolled the seat bones so that they are pointing forward towards your knees. When you arch your back, your seat bones point out behind you. When your seat bones are pointing down you will feel the roundest part of the bone on your hand.

Notice that you have a tendency to sit straighter and taller when the seat bones are pointing down (the round part of the seat bone is on your hand). That is because you have a feedback mechanism in your body that causes you to sit upright when there is pressure applied directly to the bottom of your seat bones. These sensors tell your body where you are in space and are located throughout your body especially in the joints, hands, feet, and lips. As pressure is applied to the bottom of the seat bones the body automatically responds by lengthening upward. (Interestingly enough, there are proprioceptors in the horse's feet, which tell the horse where his feet are in space. If a horse's feet are not properly trimmed or shod, this mechanism can be adversely affected which means that the horse may have difficulty knowing where to place his feet.)

When the seat bones are pointed straight down, the pelvis comes into a neutral position allowing the body to lengthen upward. This lengthening will cause an engagement of the hamstring muscles (provided the rider's leg is placed underneath her seat). The hamstring muscles cover the seat bones and slightly lift them so that the seat bones are not digging into the saddle or the horse's back. The activation of the hamstring muscles is similar to the horse engaging his hindquarters to walk forward.

The degree of engagement of the rider's seat is dependent upon the level of activity she is doing. However it is important that the pelvis operates around a neutral position so that the rider can use subtle aids rather than rough, exaggerated aids due to poor alignment. In other words, when you operate from a place of balance and alignment you can be very refined with your aids. When you are out of alignment you will have to use much more force because you have contributed to the horse's inability to respond by adding to his stiffness and lack of balance.

The neutral pelvic position also provides greater freedom of movement in the hip joint. In fact, there is a ligament that attaches the femur (thigh bone) to the pelvis. This ligament relaxes *only* when the pelvis is in a neutral position. When the pelvis is tipped forward or back, this ligament tightens and causes the leg to draw up toward the chest. So if you have been trying to lengthen your leg downward it would be extremely helpful to make sure your pelvis is in a neutral position first. A neutral position will allow the hip joints to move freely in the sockets and release tension in the leg muscles. Decreased muscle tension permits the leg to drape down through the thigh and heel which is critical to feeling and following the motion of the horse. Then you will be using only the appropriate amount of muscle tone to apply your aids rather than squishing a grape with a nutcracker.

Freeing up the hip joints allows your legs to hang properly and provides you with one of the major shock absorbers in the body. If the hip joints are restricted in any way, the ability to ride out a buck is severely compromised. Instead of absorbing the horse's motion in the joints, muscles have to start doing the work, which means gripping and/or bracing (pushing hard against the tack). Gripping increases tension in the rider's body and in the already worried horse. Unless a rider is very strong and/or very practiced in the technique of gripping with the inner thigh, knee, and/or calf, the outcome is much more likely to be a separation of the rider from his horse. When the leg joints are free and mobile the motion of the horse is taken up by the joints instead of the lower back and spine. This is also true when riding over jumps or traveling cross-country. Using your shock-absorbing joints to take up the motion takes the pounding away from both your back and your horse's back.

Bracing against the stirrup is another common posture seen in riders on young horses or when the rider is "ready" for the horse to do something. Pushing the heels down hard against the stirrup creates a rigid leg, a pivot point at the knee and/or ankle as well as stiffening the hip joint. Bracing the ankle creates a huge amount of torque (a twisting force), since the entire length of the leg becomes a lever arm. Hence, even a little amount of force applied by the horse will have a far greater effect against a rider who is bracing than one who is not.

This is not to say that people don't successfully use both of these techniques all the time. My point here is that it takes a greater amount of effort and skill when bracing and gripping than when riding with supple joints and strength in the torso. In addition, the gripping and bracing often create bigger

This rider is bracing his leg against the stirrup—notice the horse's hollow back and neck carriage.

When the leg is not braced against the stirrup, the joints can absorb the movement of the horse.

problems because the horse is reacting to the tension in the rider. The unconscious habits riders develop trying to protect themselves invariably contribute to the problem in the first place.

As an illustration of how stiffening the hip, knee, and ankle joints affect the rider's ability to easily maintain a deep seat, think about a clothespin for a minute. Remember the old wooden ones that were straight and

very rigid? You could not put very many clothes under one of these pins especially if the clothesline was a bit thick. When a strong breeze came along the motion of the line caused the clothespin to ride up and pop off. All the clothes wound up on the ground dirty again or dragged away by the neighbor's puppy. Then someone manufactured a wooden clothespin with a spring in it. This was an improvement but the best change came when plastic clothespins were invented. These are flexible enough that you can pin more clothes underneath them and they give a little. Plastic clothespins don't ride up and pop off the line like the old wooden ones. If you think about your pelvis and thighs being like a clothespin then you will see that a tight-gripping thigh or braced joints are more likely to cause you to "ride up" and pop off like the wooden clothespin. It would be preferable to be more like the plastic, hinged clothespin—a flexible seat with giving joints that will allow you to stay down in the saddle.

To get a feel of what a tight hip joint would be like to a horse's back here is a little exercise you can do with someone. Be careful. You will be surprised at how unpleasant this can be and you would not want your "friend" to be forced into her "fight" reaction.

Have one person be the "horse" and the other the "rider." The person who is the horse is going to move her forearm and hand in an up, down, and sideways motion to simulate a bucking horse. The person simulating the rider places the palm of her hand on the back of the horse's hand. The rider needs to make her wrist rigid, simulating tight hip joints. Now have the horse buck. What happens to the rider's ability to follow the horse? How does it feel to be the horse? What would the horse like to do to the rider?

Next have the rider soften the wrist—make it pretty limp. Remember that the wrist represents the hip joint. Again the rider places her palm onto the back of the horse. Have the horse buck again. Notice the difference. If you have done this exercise correctly the rider will now be able to follow the horse with a minimum of effort. It will almost feel like the rider adheres to the horse's back whereas when the rider was rigid, it was almost impossible to stay with the horse and every time the rider comes down onto the horse's back (lands on the person's hand) it hurts. So the horse wants to buck harder to remove this thing that is causing pain. You can experiment with going from a rider with a tight wrist to a limp wrist as the horse is bucking and see if you can change the behavior of the horse (i.e., lessen the bucking unconsciously because you have decreased the discomfort). This is also good practice to see if you can consciously decrease the amount of tension in your wrist during the exercise.

So if safety and security are what you are looking for, consider whether you are working against your horse or with him. Having a soft receptive seat that allows the horse to come up underneath you will be much more comforting and reassuring to the horse than one that is pounding and rigid. The depth of your seat is dependent upon how well you can release the hip joints (allow them to move) rather than how firmly you can grip. If you are bracing then it is more likely that the horse will find you uncomfortable and therefore be worried rather than reassured when things get a bit tense. However, this takes practice since it is human instinct to hold and grip when we get scared. It is our form of "flight" reflex.

We have to train ourselves to let go and allow our body to follow the motion of the horse rather than fight it. In order to speed

This rider is not braced against the stirrup. There is depth in the heel without pushing the leg forward. Notice the even leg contact with the horse.

This rider is bracing against her stirrup. Notice that her leg has swung forward and there is very little leg contact with the horse.

up this process you can develop awareness of your body so that you can consciously override your flight reflex by breathing and softening in the hips. To do this you must first start with the understanding of what you are trying to achieve and then the awareness of the habit pattern you are currently in. By developing this awareness and experimenting with different body movements you will be able to create new patterns of movement and take action rather than operating from old reactive patterns.

Next time you go for a ride, consciously bring your attention to your pelvis and hip joints. Notice how they are moving (or not moving) on the saddle. Does it feel like they can follow the horse's motion or do they feel stuck? Do the two joints feel the same? When you are off the horse, test out your range of motion in your hips. I have actually seen people who can put their feet behind their head. Fortunately, this level of flexibility is not required for good riding!

However, it is important that there is some degree of freedom in your hips, knees, and ankles. Gently explore the range of motion of each of these joints. By simply observing what your range of motion is, you can begin to increase it. It is important not to force the body in this type of exercise. Simply explore how easy it is to move the joints in all ranges of motion. If you find that it is limited in any particular direction do less and just move the joints. If you force the range of motion you have only focused on the limitation rather than the potential available to you.

By practicing the movements very slowly and minutely at first, you will begin to send messages through the nervous system to the brain. As this happens (and it is critical here that you do this without causing any pain!) the brain starts looking at the possibility of motion rather than the limitation. If you force the motion and cause pain, the brain is no longer capable of learning the new movement.

Discovering more about how your body moves (and doesn't move) without judgment can go a long way toward developing a deeper more secure seat. The simple act of developing an awareness of the range of motion in your leg joints will begin the process of change so that ultimately you can be relaxed and comfortable while riding. By finding a neutral pelvis, engaging the postural support mechanism, mobilizing your hip joints, and lessening the tension in your legs, your seat will naturally deepen in the saddle. Practice these concepts on a quiet horse to train yourself in the new habit patterns. This will provide you with the foundation of an unconscious habit pattern later on. Hopefully, with a little practice, the next time you really need it you can call upon your soft hip joints to ride through the difficulty and remain partnered with your horse.

The Feldenkrais method® is an excellent way to learn how to move with greater ease and less effort. For more information about the Feldenkrais method, to find classes, or a practitioner check out www. Feldenkrais.com.

12

Hip Joints

EXERCISES FOR YOUR HORSE SUCH AS LOWERING THE HEAD, RAISING THE back with belly lifts, and pelvic tilts all encourage the horse to lengthen the topline (the distance from the poll to the dock), engage the abdominal muscles, and connect the front end to back end. Lengthening the horse's topline allows him to bring the hindquarters under so that he can track up (hind foot stepping into the print of the front foot). With the hind feet tracking up, the thrust from the hind feet will

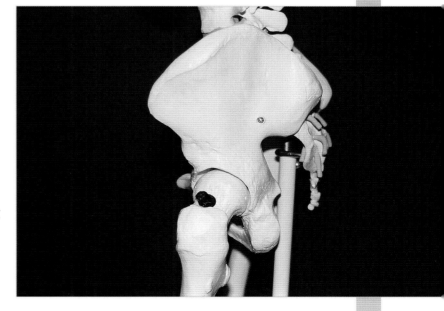

Notice in this side view of hip joint and pelvis the end of the sacrum and tailbone coming down from the spine and the seat bone below the hip joint.

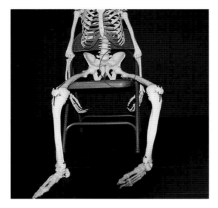 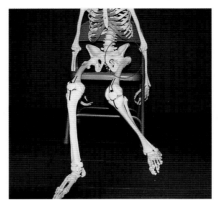 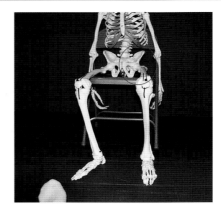

In addition to arching and rounding the back, riding with your foot rolled either to the outside or inside on the stirrup will also restrict the hip joints. Rolling to the outside of the foot takes your knee away from the side of the horse and restricts the back of the hip joint (left). The distance between the greater trochanter (knob on the side of the thighbone at the top) to the seat bone is reduced at the back. Rolling to the inside of the foot causes you to knee pinch and restricts the front of the hip joint by reducing the distance between the seat bone and the greater trochanter circled area on the front side of the seat bone (middle). In both the pelvis is no longer able to glide freely forward. When the foot is flat and the knee is lined up over the foot (right). The distance between the greater trochanter and the seat bone is at its maximum allowing the most room for the horse's back to come up into the rider's seat.

help lift the back, provide balancing support for down transitions, and make the horse's job of carrying the rider's weight a lot easier. If the rider (or saddle) blocks the horse from lifting the back, the horse will either go above the bit or behind the bit in order to avoid discomfort.

Most often riders cause the horse to hollow his back or go behind the bit because they are contracted through their topline (top of head to tail bone) and tight in the hips. Riding with equipment such as a neck rope (see Chapter 22) helps riders to release the hips so that the horse can move more comfortably with his back relaxed. If you have ever seen a rider unable to work with a neck rope, it is often because the rider is gripping or driving with her legs and is braced through the hips and back. If the rider is hollow-backed and bracing or

Here, Andy's back is in resting position.

I am asking Andy to lift his back. Notice the engagement of his abdominal muscles and that he has lowered his head.

Equine version of a pelvic tilt. Andy is extremely flexible and can do this without discomfort. However, most horses are not this flexible and this could be quite uncomfortable for them. Therefore, you must use extreme caution when asking a horse to tilt his pelvis like this.

I am showing a group of students how to locate their hip joints.

slumped into a "c" curve, the hip joint will also be restricted.

In order to understand the effect of the hips and pelvis we need to start with a brief anatomy lesson. The hip joints are ball-and-socket joints. The socket is part of the pelvis while the ball is at the end of your thigh-bone or femur. At the top of the femur the bone angles in (the neck of the femur) and the ball is on top. Therefore the ball angles into the socket of the pelvis (Fig. 1). The sockets lie at an angle in the pelvis with the seat bones (*ischial tuberosities*) lying between them. The sacrum is the fused part of the spine that connects to the pelvis and the tail-bone or coccyx is at the end of the sacrum.

Many people do not understand where their hip joints are. To find your hips joints start by standing up and pointing one foot towards the ground directly underneath you. This will cause a crease in your pants in the groin area. If you follow the thigh up towards the top of the leg where it meets the torso, you will feel a large rubber-band like structure or tendon. This tendon is part of one of the quadriceps muscle of the thigh. Feel towards the inside of this tendon and as far in as you comfortably can back towards your sacrum and you will approach your hip joint. Notice how deep it is within your body. Now keeping your hand there rotate

your leg still pointing your toe on the ground to move the ball in the socket. You will get a sense of how far in your hip sockets are. Take your other hand and reach back to your sacrum on the same side. The sacrum feels like a large flat triangle with the tailbone hanging off the bottom point. Notice that there are two dimples in the sacrum (one on each side) about 1.5" from the midline. (Everyone has these dimples and regardless of how fat or thin you are you can find them.) Place your index finger in the dimple on the same side of the pelvis as your hand in front. Now move your hip again and think of a line running from your front hand to your back finger. This is the diagonal line that the hip joint lies on.

Sit down again and notice if you folded at your hips to sit or rounded in your waist. When you slump in a chair the hips lose the fold at the front. If you arch your back sitting in the chair, there is too much fold at the front. Find your seat bones pointing straight down through the chair and notice how much angle there is at the front of the hip. Place one hand on your lower back, just below your belt line, to be sure that you are not hollowing or arching your back. Wobble your legs back and forth and notice

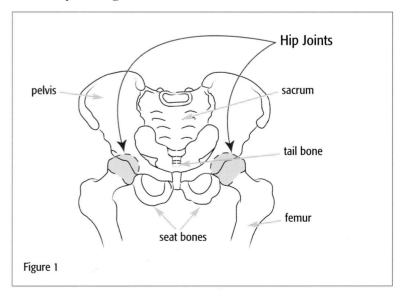

Figure 1

the feeling in your hip sockets. Of course when you are sitting in a chair your legs are out in front of you rather than directly underneath you as in a saddle. But for now it helps you get an idea of what it is like to let the hip move in the socket in a seated position.

Next, think about butt walking. Remember when you were a kid and you would sit on the floor and move yourself along by scooting each side of your pelvis forward on the floor? When you think about doing this on the chair notice whether you want to lift the pelvis up to move it forward or if you can simply slide the pelvis forward. You want to be able to slide without much lifting. Observe how the knee on the side you are moving advances over your foot. In order for this to happen you have to allow the knees to go out over your second toe. If you pinch your knees together you will not be able to butt walk. Instead you will simply waddle side to side. You can butt walk yourself to the edge of the chair and back again as long as the chair has a fairly level, flat surface. (Be careful not to butt walk off the edge of the chair!) By "butt walking" on the chair backwards you can get the feeling of letting the ball of the hip joint sink back into the socket. This is an important feeling to remember when riding. Oftentimes when we are on the horse the ball of the hip joint gets pressed against the front of the socket. This can cause the horse to stiffen and rush. By letting the ball move towards the back of the socket (this is a very small movement) the hip joint softens and the horse can slow down or shift his balance onto his hindquarters.

Finally stand up again and do the following exercise. This exercise will show you the importance of having your pelvis in a neutral position so that your hips can move freely. It also demonstrates what happens to the horse's hips and his ability to track up depending upon the angle of his pelvis. Remember to be gentle with your body during all of these exercises. If anything causes you pain—stop! These exercises are simply to give you and understanding of a concept, not to hurt you.

Start by standing up. Now assume the posture of a rider with an arched back or a head-high, hollow-backed horse standing up (same thing actually). Now pick up one knee and notice how easy or difficult it is for you to raise your leg (Fig. 2). Did you have to shift your weight to the other leg? How much did you shift? How easy is it to sustain this position? Put your leg down and assume a "c" curve rider position (same as horse behind the bit). Get good and slumped. Notice that you have flattened the crease of your hip joints when you slump. Again, pick up one leg. Notice how difficult or easy it is and how you have to redistribute your weight in order to lift the knee. Finally, find a neutral pelvic position with your seat bones pointing down towards the ground and your sacrum hanging down. Feel your lower back to make sure it is not rounded or arched. Pick up your knee again. How easy or difficult was it? Did you notice that you did not have to shift your weight nearly so much in order to pick up your knee?

Compare the different positions; hollow back, "c" curve, and neutral in relation to picking up one knee. Which position took the least amount of effort? If you said the neutral position then I agree with you, as do all of my students. When the pelvis is in a neutral position the ligament that runs between the pelvis and the femur releases. This reduces the tension in the hip joint making it easier to lift the leg. Notice that in the hollow-back position the sacrum is tipped up so that the pelvis pitches forward and down. In the "c" curve position there is very little fold in the hip joint and you wind

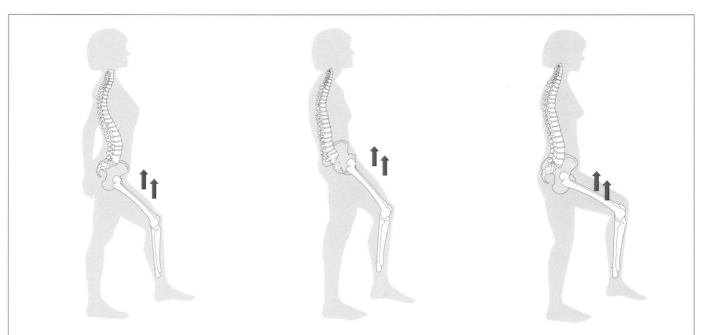

Figure 2. Different postures and their effect on being able to lift your leg up. Hollow back—notice that the knee does not come up very far (left). "C" curve or rounded back posture. The knee has not come up much more than the hollow posture (middle). Neutral position—notice that the knee has easily come up to parallel with the ground (right).

Hollow: Fran can't lift her leg very high.

"c" curve: Fran's leg is still restricted.

Neutral: Notice how much higher Fran can lift her leg with ease.

up bending at the waist which inhibits the movement in the hip joint.

If you consider the horse for a moment you will realize that if he is behind or above the bit (as you just simulated) it will be harder for him to track up than when he is on the bit (back up, pelvis under, release in hip joints). He will have to work through the resistance in the hip joints just like you felt in your own hip joints. Many horses are driven through this resistance. However, if you get the horse to lengthen his top line he will have an effortless swing in the hind legs instead of you always having to drive him on.

Returning to the standing exercise, if you fold the joints of hip, knee, and ankle of the supporting leg with the pelvis in a neutral position, it is still easy to lift the knee. You might notice that you have tucked your pelvis under you a bit more as you folded the leg joints. This is similar to what happens to the horse in a more collected frame; the hindquarters lower and the hips are still free to come under. Do this again with a hollow back or a "c" curve back and notice that there is a great deal of strain placed on your knees (horse's stifles) and it is difficult to hold your balance for any length of time. Next time you watch someone riding in collection consider whether the horse is lowering his pelvis to do it or if he is stiffening.

You will know how that feels now that you have experimented.

Hopefully you now have a much clearer idea about your hip joints, pelvis, and how they work. Next time you ride your horse, place your hand on your lower back. Observe which position your pelvis is in; hollow, "c" curve or flat. If you have constantly been struggling to get your leg longer by lengthening your stirrups and you notice that your back is hollow, I suggest you shorten your stirrups a hole or two. Once you are able to keep the back full by developing the proper muscle strength in the back, go ahead and let your stirrups down gradually again. You will find that you will be able to keep your feet where they belong even at the longer length once you have strengthened your back to maintain the pelvis in a neutral position. Also notice that your leg hangs more freely. Play with the idea of the ball moving back into the socket to slow the horse down. As you become more aware of your hip joints notice what happens to your horse's movement. Does his stride increase? Are down transitions easier? Can you maintain your sitting trot with less effort? So much of riding is centered around the hips, pelvis, and lower back, I promise that any effort you make to become more aware of this part of your body will help improve your riding.

13

Are You Really Sitting Tall in the Saddle?

IN THIS CHAPTER, WE WILL LOOK AT A COUPLE OF PHOTOS OF GENNIE, WHICH were taken at a clinic in Kent, Washington. Before we actually look at the pictures, let me explain the purpose of this discussion.

WHAT YOU WILL LEARN

My intent is to provide you with some images, explanations, and suggestions that will give you insights into your own riding. For those visual learners out there, you may find yourself saying, "Yeah, I do that too!" By identifying with the photos, I am hoping

that you will be able to use the suggestions that follow to improve your own riding.

In the analysis of each photo I am also going to include a description of how the rider's posture is affecting the horse. The purpose of this is for you to become more aware of the relationship between the rider's position and horse's "use of self." The horse, in this regard, serves as a mirror for what the rider is doing. I have taken the images and drawn lines on them to illustrate my point.

IMPERFECTION IS THE RULE

One thing we need to keep in mind here is that there is no perfectly symmetrical human or horse. All you have to do is look out into the paddock at a herd of horses or at a bunch of people in the mall to realize this fact. The perfectly conformed horse or person is extremely rare if they exist at all. This alone dictates that there will be asymmetries in horses and humans not to mention throwing a fixed object (the saddle) between the two asymmetrical moving objects. In looking at hundreds of saddles (both Western and English), it is rare that I find a straight one. Some saddles are better than others but needless to say a crooked saddle is going to affect the straightness of both the horse and the rider to some degree depending on the severity of the twist. This is often the cause of a severe brace in the back.

HOW PATTERNS GET SET

In addition to basic conformation, consider what we do to our bodies all day long. Every time we have an injury (both human and horse), however slight, we develop a brace or a compensatory pattern of movement. These patterns become rapidly ingrained within us most often without our awareness and compound the underlying

issues we were born with. Think about the last time you smashed your finger. How long did it take for you to use that hand again? In the meantime your body held itself differently and you guarded the injured hand. During that time the proprioceptors (those cellular mechanisms that tell you where you are in space) in your muscles and joints altered to the different pattern of movement. Unless those proprioceptors are reset (like your microwave clock after the power has gone off) they will continue to function with some degree of the new pattern of restriction you have developed. Over time this pattern dictates how you use your entire body. This process is like twisting a towel; you keep winding around the end you are holding until the entire towel is twisted in a ball.

Horses have this same proprioceptive mechanism occurring in their bodies. In addition, they will unconsciously react to the restrictions in the human by altering their movement. All you have to do is watch the same horse being ridden by two different riders to see this. The horse will automatically adapt to the feel of the rider, whatever the rider is doing consciously or otherwise. The horse's reaction to the rider will depend on the psychological makeup of that individual horse. A school horse most likely will shut down when he feels someone who is tight and stiff. A green colt might attempt to run away.

Good riders are capable of overriding the horse's response to their restriction in movement. Most natural riders don't even realize that they have felt the restriction in the horse and dealt with it without ever considering that they might have caused it in the first place. If they were to address the restriction in themselves first however, they might not have had to deal with it in the horse at all.

CHANGING THE PATTERNS

Unless we address these patterns we continue to limit our range of motion and repeatedly deal with the same restriction which adversely affects our horses and our riding. By becoming aware of these habit patterns we can change and improve the quality of our movement, our horse's movement, and our partnership together. It is the rare person who is the natural rider and never has to consider these things. It is the majority that must address this in order to improve.

Remember that both people and horses come together with their own set of physical issues, which, if nothing else, are the result of their conformation. Simply being alive means that there are going to be patterns that we can work on. So these photos don't show perfection. I want the photos to give you some insights as to why you may be having difficulty accomplishing certain tasks with your horse like a round circle or a steady trot. Hopefully then you will be able to discover ways to improve.

THE GOAL

Ultimately the goal (if there is one) of this process is to restore the horse to his natural movement in spite of the rider on his back. In fact, I believe we can exceed this goal through working in partnership. My goal is to create a quality of movement, sense of self, and enjoyment in both the horse and rider that is greater than what they could experience on their own because of their relationship with each other. By preserving the potential in either we unlock the creative process in both so that they can create something more together.

In the end I hope you realize your personal best as expressed by the comfort and ease of your horse when he is carrying you on his back. It may take an entire lifetime to get close to your ideal and it may not be

perfection in someone else's eyes, but that doesn't matter. What does matter is that you continually work on becoming aware of the unconscious habits that inhibit your riding and your horses, accept them for now, and work toward changing them. I suggest you find someone whose riding you admire. Model that in your own mind. At the same time allow your own creative nature to help find ways to achieve your ideal and possibly even surpass it. During this process your horse will continue to serve as the mirror of your development telling you when you are doing better or worse. By simply acknowledging the horse for his patience, allow yourself the opportunity to learn and be open to different ideas. Fortunately horses are more forgiving of our mistakes than we are and will tolerate our learning process. Perhaps there is something to be learned in this as well.

PHOTO 1

The first thing I notice in Photo 1 is the straight line from Gennie's shoulders through her hips. This tells me that her pelvis is underneath her and her back is

Photo 1. Gennie traveling to the left.

long at the waist. The waist area is equivalent to the horse's loins. Her breathing appears to be in her abdomen (a good thing). However, when we add a line through the ear, shoulder, hip, and ankle it becomes obvious that her head and feet are in front of the line of gravity. This is a result of tightness in the hip joints and neck. Notice that the horse is also hollow in the neck and is not stepping up underneath Gennie. Her eyes are focused down toward the ground on the inside which has caused her to drop her left (inside) shoulder. Looking down is going to drop her head even further forward of the vertical line and be potentially dangerous if the horse should stumble or fall because she will pitch forward over the inside shoulder. Notice that the horse is dropping in on the inside shoulder as well.

PHOTO 2

In Photo 2, Gennie's eyes are up and she looks confident of the line she is riding (she appears to have a plan and is directing her horse). The line through her ear, shoulder,

Photo 2. Gennie traveling to the right.

hip, and ankle is better. The horse is brighter, rounder in the neck, and has a more eager look on his face. However, notice the hollow place in her lower back at the waist. This could be contributing to the tension I observe in her shoulders and arms. Also notice that her rib cage on the right is collapsing a bit which is causing her shoulders to be unlevel.

When I compare these two photos it appears to me that the ground seat in Gennie's saddle may be too wide for her. In the first photo she has her back straight but her legs want to pull forward and up from the hip. In the second photo her legs are more underneath her but her back is hollow. This is a typical of a ground seat that is too wide (a common problem I see with some Western saddles). The rider is unable to free her hips and have her legs hang underneath her. It is like straddling a stool that is too wide. In order to accommodate the ground seat and place the leg underneath, the rider must tip her pelvis forward and down thus restricting her hip joints. If she levels the pelvis the wide ground seat pushes her leg forward and up preventing her from having good alignment and grounding through the feet.

When the hips are restricted it is difficult to increase the energy in the rider's body and the horse. Notice that in both photos the horse is not moving forward freely nor is he coming underneath himself from behind resulting in his weight falling on the forehand. In other words, he is also restricted in the hip joints so he is not able to track up underneath himself.

If you, like Gennie in this photo, are dealing with a saddle with a ground seat that is too wide, releasing your hip will help you deal with the width. Make sure that your pelvis is level in the saddle (as in Photo 1). Find your seat bones pointing straight down. Begin by breathing into the pelvis and hips. Take your feet out of the stirrups and raise your knees up to help find the seat bones. Make small circles with your ankles rotating in both directions. Gradually let your legs come down. Finish with internally rotating circles.

I would suggest that you rise to the trot keeping your pelvis underneath you so that you open up in the hip joints. Make sure you are rising on the outside foreleg. Then think of the rising phase of the trot being longer than the sitting phase. This will open your hips and allow your horse to step deeper under you with the inside hind leg because you are "creating space" for it. By having the horse step deeper, there will be more support for your pelvis and you will find it easier to keep your leg underneath you. This will also lighten the horse off the forehand and will be a more enjoyable ride for both of you. Once the horse is moving forward more freely and your hips have let go, return to the sitting trot and notice that it will be much lighter and easier.

By the way, these photos of Gennie were taken in 1999. I worked with her again in 2003 and her riding is very much improved! I appreciate riders like Gennie who help me learn and who are willing to help us all learn by letting me examine their riding.

Supporting Your Horse Through the Leg and Seat

*I*N THE PHOTOS IN THIS CHAPTER WE ARE GOING TO EXAMINE WHETHER THE riders are supporting their horses through the leg and seat. As we look at each picture notice the statement on the horse's face, where the tension is in the horse's body, and how the rider is influencing the horse (good or bad). Which ones look like the rider is in harmony with the horse and which do not? Look for what is good in each photo. Often this is harder than looking for what's not so good because we are so accustomed to criticizing.

Recently I have begun my lessons by asking my students what they do well. They hem and haw and "um" for a while and then try to spit something out. But if I ask them what they do badly they answer immediately with a list. I find it interesting that we view our riding by our inabilities rather than our abilities. Ask yourself what is different in each photo that justifies your decision. Then ask yourself "What could the rider do differently?" Also consider how the rider's position is influencing the horse so that when you are riding and you feel your horse doing something similar to what you saw in these photos, you have some idea what you can do to help your horse go better.

Photo 1

PHOTO 1

This rider's right leg is severely turned out with the heel locked down which will restrict the hip joint. His upper body is pretty good with the shoulder over the hip and the elbow in a good position relative to his hip. However, the outwardly rotated leg is going to prevent his pelvis from following the forward motion of the horse and block the outside hind of the horse from coming under. The rider is looking down and collapsing on the left side as he tries to flex the horse to the left. The horse is falling through the outside shoulder and the inside hind leg is not going to be able to step up underneath the rider's weight. Therefore, this horse is going to have a hard time catching himself and will continue to fall on the forehand. Notice that the running martingale is not being used but its existence indicates that this rider has had a problem with this horse's headset. I would have preferred to see it tied up so that it did not hit the horse in the legs while it was not in use. However, the bigger issue is why he needs the martingale in the first place. If the rider brought his leg back underneath him with his feet pointing forward the horse

could step underneath himself more easily. As the hind leg comes further under the body the horse will be able to lift his back and release his head and neck down eliminating the need for the running martingale.

PHOTO 2

Again we have a rider bracing against his stirrups. However, in this photo he has allowed the horse to use his head and neck freely by letting go of the reins. The horse is willing to stretch out and down with his neck showing a nice release of the under-neck muscles. Notice that this saddle is too small for this rider and too short for the horse. Even if the rider brought his leg back underneath, he is still sitting on the cantle. His upper body is tipping forward to balance over his feet thus putting the horse on the forehand. All of the rider's weight is pressing down on the horse's back at the lowest point instead of distributing weight along the entire span of the rib cage. There is no upward support from the rider's lower leg because it is out in front. Therefore, the horse will hollow his back out and not be able to step underneath the rider easily. Observe how the horse appears to be higher in the croup and

Photo 2

falling out through the sternum. If the horse were allowed to take a deeper step behind then he would lift the rider up and carry more weight on the hindquarters. In order to help this situation I would find a longer saddle that spans the length of the horse's rib cage and provided enough room to accommodate the rider without parking him on the cantle. Then I would bring the rider's leg back underneath him and have him support his seat through his lower leg, thus encouraging the horse to take a deeper step behind.

Photo 3

PHOTO 3

In this photo we see issues similar to photos 1 and 2 only now we are moving at a lope. Everything you see in the walk will compound itself the faster the horse goes. I like the way this rider is using his eyes. He is looking where he is going. It seems like he has a plan. While he has contact on the horse's mouth, he is not pulling back. Instead he has allowed his elbows to come forward to make up for the short reins. Looking at the equipment on this horse's head I would guess that the rider has problems keeping the horse's head down. Again, let's ask the question why.

First of all, the rider's legs are out in front of him. So there is not upward support from the leg to the seat. Again, this means that all of the rider's weight is pressing down onto the horse's back. The rider is rounded in the shoulders and back, which restricts his hips. The greater the restriction in the rider's hips, the greater the degree of difficulty for the horse to engage his hindquarters. As the hindquarters drift further out behind, more and more weight falls onto the forehand. Notice also that the rider is leaning in on the turn following the horse as he falls in on the shoulder, which will cause the horse to lean even more. The tie-down is to stop the horse from raising his head—in an effort to stop falling forward, the horse will naturally raise his head. This makes sense when you figure that as the horse raises his head he physically shifts the weight more toward the hindquarters. While this is not the solution we want the horse to pick, it is a logical choice biomechanically when the horse can't lift the back to shift the weight rearward.

If the rider were to bring his leg back underneath him, open across the collarbones, and lengthen the reins, the horse could come off the forehand. Conversely if the rider were to take a forward seat over his feet (since his reins are so short), then the horse would again be able to come up in the back and shift his weight to the hindquarters without having to raise his head.

PHOTO 4

Photo 4

In this photo the rider is sitting in a very balanced position. Notice that he is square through the body. The collarbones are wide and open. His back is straight but not rigid. Neither horse nor rider is leaning through the turn. The rider's legs are hanging down into the stirrups and the weight of the rider's leg is balanced in the stirrup. The horse has a pleasant look on his face and he is carrying himself with a "weight of rein" contact. While the rider's leg is not directly underneath his seat, the fender is hanging straight down. This means that the rider is not bracing against the stirrup. The overall impression is that this rider is carrying himself instead of letting the horse bear the entire weight on his back. The rider's pelvis is in a neutral position and the horse is bending nicely around the rider's inside leg through the turn. There is a sense of upward forward impulsion and relaxation in both horse and rider. Notice that the horse is lifting through the withers which allows the head and neck to lengthen from the base. Any downward pressure on the withers will block this motion and cause the horse to hollow out. Lifting in the withers is critical to coming off the forehand, especially in the canter, where the natural undulation of the spine is to lift up. When comparing these photos notice that the horse with the greatest degree of relaxation has the rider who demonstrates the best overall balance and ease. By establishing a correct position, the rider can assist the horse in finding a comfortable place to be. If the rider pushes the lower leg forward then all the rider's weight comes down onto the horse's back and causes the horse to hollow and fall further onto the fore-

hand. When the rider's lower leg remains underneath his seat, the lower leg can upwardly support the weight of the rider and help the horse lift up through the back. This lower leg support will also allow the rider's chest and shoulders to open because they no longer curl forward in an effort to place the body weight over the feet. As the chest and shoulders open, the hips free up, and the horse can take a deeper step behind which helps lighten the forehand.

Next time, before you mount, take up the same position you would have in the saddle. If you ride with your feet out in front of you, stand rocked back on your heels with your feet ahead of your body. Make sure you drive your heels down when you do this. What is the first thing you want to do? I bet your reaction was to find something to grab in order to catch yourself from falling. The only difference between doing this exercise on the ground and on horseback is that the horse is the one who suffers. He has to catch your backward fall into his back and then feel the concomitant pull on the reins. When you are balanced over your feet, the horse no longer becomes your couch. You start doing your part in carrying yourself allowing him to carry you.

15

The Power Is in the Position

POWER POSITION (THE POSITION OF GREATEST SECURITY AND strengths with the least amount of effort when I pull on the rider's reins) is proof that the classical alignment of ear, shoulder, hip, and ankle combined with diaphragmatic breathing, provides the strongest, most secure position for the rider. It also illustrates that if the rider stiffens at all, including the diaphragm, not only will her seat be less secure, the horse will wind up resisting and holding tension in the

Allie is in a forward seat "Power Position." Her correct alignment makes her strong and secure.

same part of his body. Joints are designed to move. When we restrict joints in order to achieve greater strength a pivot point is created. Instead of having a firm feeling throughout the entire muscle system ("soft feel") there is stiffness. Not only will this be tiring to the rider, it will impede the horse's ability to move freely.

Remember the exercise of shaking one hand then tightening one finger as you were shaking your hand? Not only did the finger tighten, your other fingers tightened, your wrist got stiff, and your breathing lessened or stopped. Suddenly, instead of being soft and responsive on the reins, your hands became clubs pulling on the horse's mouth. So we are looking for a position that will allow your body to have a softness rather than a stiffness and have a flow that goes through the entire body.

The way I look at it, stiffness is anything that restricts the flow of energy and firmness is when the energy can move freely throughout the entire system. Think of a hose. If the water can flow freely then whatever went in at the top of the hose is going to come out from the bottom. There is a steady even volume of water through the entire length of the system. Then put some crimps in the hose or let your horse stand on part of it. Suddenly the amount of water is greatly reduced. You may only have a trickle of water coming out. This same concept applies to electricity when there is resistance in the wiring or acupuncture which removes the blockage in the body's flow of energy or "chi," or to the horse when there is stiffness anywhere in his body especially in the neck and back. You can't really get your horse to move his feet if the horse has a 2x6 board for a neck. The muscles are rigid and block the signals from the rider's hands. There is little or no "water running through the hose" down to the horse's feet because it has been crimped in the rigid muscles in the horse's neck. Therefore, if you do exercises to remove the stiffness and improve the flow, you can improve your effortless strength.

Now think about your body. If you have fluid joints and firm (but not tense) muscles, the entire body can act in a coordinated manner from your fingertips to your feet. You have a softness in your body. You can feel the connectedness of the entire system (and as a result, the entire horse). In fact, there is an anatomical system called *fascia* that connects all of the muscles in the body in order to transfer and absorb energy. Fascia is a layer of thin opaque material that surrounds all the muscles from head to toe. It is this layer of tissue you see holding the muscles together when you pull a chicken leg apart or the whitish outer covering on a roast you notice before putting it in the oven. Fascia keeps the flow of information traveling along the muscle system to even out the tension.

So a classical alignment places the body in a position where movement can flow through the body without restriction. The joints remain supple and absorbing while the muscles provide strength. At the same time this alignment is the most effective position for using your seat to engage the horse. Remember that this position is dependent on the rider being able to start with the pelvis in a neutral position so that the hip joints can hang freely in the hip sockets.

PHOTO 1

Notice in Photo 1 that Mindy is in a very common position seen in a lot of people. If you draw a vertical line through her hips, her leg is in front of the line of gravity and her upper body is slightly behind. Notice that Mindy is demonstrating excellent use of eyes (looking ahead), her shoulders are wide and open, and she has a good line through her ear, shoulder, and hip even though this line is angled back at the top.

Photo 1

Her elbow is well placed near the top of her pelvis and you can imagine a straight line from her hands to the bit. The only major issue is that her feet are out in front of her because she is pressing forward and down into the stirrups. (Please note: There is a huge difference between pushing the lower leg and foot forward to have the appearance of the heels down and lengthening the back of the leg and ankle so that the heel drops. Many people push their leg forward in an attempt to lower their heel. Then when they bring their leg back the truth is revealed. They have never released the back of the leg

Photo 2

to lower the heels in the first place. Ankle exercises would help lengthen the back of the leg so that the heels truly go down.)

PHOTO 2

In Photo 2 I am testing to see if Mindy's usual position is strong enough to prevent me from pulling her out of the saddle. Notice that she has pivoted over her knee and therefore her upper body has come forward. She is trying to resist me using her shoulders and back but because of the pivot point created by the leg position, I can easily pull her out of the saddle. Remember that I am not nearly as strong as a horse. You can see that it did not take a lot of effort on my part to pull her forward. Also note something unusual in that Mindy is capable of maintaining her upper body alignment when I pulled.

Having tested Power Position with hundreds of people I can tell you that there is a large variation in what happens when I pull on the reins in the rider's "normal" strength position. The bottom line is that I am capable of "unseating" 90% of the riders with minimal effort. Those riders not in a vertical alignment, who I can't unseat, have spent years developing upper body and leg strength to hold them securely in place. In those cases however, the amount of effort required on the riders' part to prevent me from unseating them is enormous. I will see their biceps bulge, their breathing severely restricted, and they will ultimately fatigue and collapse. Also, when I pull on the reins, these riders move forward and up through the pelvis, which takes their seat out of the saddle instead of deepening it. And more importantly, the effect of this amount of strength on the horse causes the horse to stiffen and drop his back.

When riders are in Power Position (classical alignment), the horse brings the back up and engages the hindquarters because the rider is no longer stiffening. As I pull, the rider's seat deepens easily into the saddle. It takes a minimum amount of effort on the rider's part to maintain position. Hence, the rider can continue to breathe, stay centered, and look around in spite of my pulling on the reins because she is using a fraction of the muscle strength to resist me vs. the rider who is behind the vertical and gripping to stay put.

PHOTO 3

In Photo 3 we have placed Mindy's leg underneath her seat. Notice that in Mindy's case she has sufficient length through the back of the leg that her heel is down with her leg underneath her. There is a straight line from her hip through her ankle. Mindy is still slightly behind the vertical with her upper body as a result of her pelvis being tipped back slightly in a rounded position. To correct this she would need to fold slightly from the hip joint which would bring her entire upper body forward. Her upper body has maintained the good position we saw in the first photo in terms of the openness in the shoulders, her elbow placement, her use of eyes, and the straight line from elbow to bit.

PHOTO 4

In Photo 4 I am testing out Mindy's new Power Position. Notice that I am exerting a much greater amount of effort to no avail. Mindy is securely in the saddle with no bracing or pivot points to rotate over. Her muscles and joints are absorbing the force of my pull. In fact the harder I pull, the deeper Mindy's seat is drawn down into the saddle because there is no stiffening in her joints. Observe that since she was not perfectly straight through the upper body to begin with, she has had to lean back slightly. If she had been totally vertical through her pelvis and upper body she would not have had to lean.

Notice that I am not pulling on the horse's mouth during this exercise since I

Photo 3

Photo 4

have taken the reins behind the bit and am pulling down, toward the horse's mouth.

PHOTO 5

In Photo 5 I am again pulling on Mindy while she is in Power Position. By remaining soft in the knee, Mindy's lower leg has closed on the horse's sides causing the horse to walk toward me. Mindy's body weight is now borne throughout her entire leg so that there is less downward force onto the horse's back. This allows the horse to come up in the back rather than drop away from her seat that results when the leg is being pushed in front of the

Photo 5

So next time you are in the saddle consider whether you are pushing your feet and legs out in front of you getting "prepared" for the worst or whether your legs are hanging easily underneath you gently supporting your horse. On a quiet, steady horse, notice what happens to your overall balance when you bring your legs under your seat. Experiment with the two different leg positions (out in front and underneath) feeling the difference in the horse's movement and willingness to go forward. You may be surprised to find that your horse is much happier and more willing to move when you have "taken your feet off the dashboards" and support yourself through your lower body by having your legs under you. Also, you might find that suddenly all those achy knees and sore feet you have been complaining about on long rides have disappeared.

This exercise is something I teach at all of my clinics and was developed by my associate Allie Thurston of Easton, CT. For those of you familiar with "the Buttress" exercise in *Centered Riding*, this is the equivalent performed on horseback. (For more information on the Buttress, please refer to Sally Swift's book, *Centered Riding*.)

line of gravity. By letting her calf close gently on the horse's sides, Mindy is engaging the horse to move forward into the contact rather than resist. Think of it like giving the horse a hug through the midsection and sending it forward. As the rib cage comes up and the hind leg steps under, the horse will be able to lengthen the head and neck and establish a soft contact with the bit. The rider then becomes the balancing fulcrum around which the horse moves. Hindquarters connect to the bridle because the bridge through the middle has been established allowing energy to flow freely from one end to the other.

Here, Allie is demonstrating a variety of very insecure jumping positions. I can easily pull her forward in the first three (from left to right) knee pinching, lower leg jammed forward, and round backed. In the last photo she is also insecure and is almost laying on the horse's neck. Notice how the horse has hollowed her back as a result.

16

Lateral Balance in the Saddle

W̲E HAVE BEEN SPENDING QUITE A BIT OF TIME LOOKING AT RIDers from the side so I thought it would be a nice change to look from a different angle. This chapter shows a series of photos taken from the back. As an instructor I find it really important to spend time standing on the outside of the circle. There

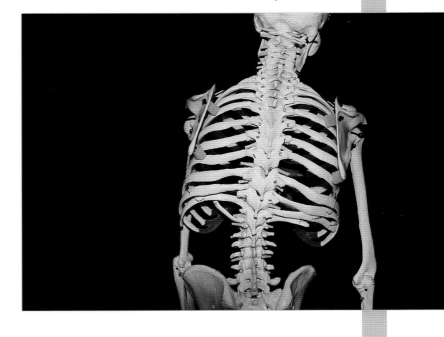

is so much you can miss if you only stand in the middle of the ring and look at your students from the side. When you stand near

This skeleton's spine is curving to the right. Notice the low right shoulder and rotation left in the pelvis. Observe that the right arm is hanging away from the body while the left arm is close to the ribs.

the fence, the student has to find his or her own line instead of relying on you for a reference point. This is similar to riding in the open versus an arena where the horse leans on the wall. I watch my students from the outside so I can see both sides as they go around a circle. I also have them travel down a line directly away from me so I can observe their lateral balance.

If the rider is sitting with one side of the rib cage collapsed then his weight distribution will not be even across the saddle. As an example of this, sit in a fairly firm chair with a level seat. Now collapse one side of your rib cage. Notice where you are sitting on your seat bones. Do you feel more weight on the seat bone opposite to the collapsed ribs or on the same side? Everyone will react a bit differently. Generally you will feel more weight on the seat bone opposite to the collapsed side. Some people feel more weight on the same side. Now collapse on the opposite side and notice if it is harder or easier to collapse your ribs. Where has the weight gone now? What happens to your breathing? Where does your head go?

In either case, when the rib cage is not evenly lengthened from the top of the pelvis to just underneath the shoulder girdle, you will wind up putting more weight on one seat bone. Your head will naturally drop to one side and your breathing will be restricted because the rib cage cannot expand evenly. Once you have tilted to the side, you are no longer in line with the action of gravity. You will have to use muscle to keep from falling off the horse. As we have already explored, unwanted muscle tension restricts movement in both you and your horse.

Now think about what collapsing your weight over to one side does to your horse. Here you are sitting heavier on one side of your saddle. This is going to pull the saddle off center and possibly shift the bars or pan-

els of the saddle across the horse's spine. The horse's spine is not designed to bear weight so your horse will have to drop his back down to avoid the pain. If the weight shift is only slight it may be a cue for your horse to respond in a certain way. He may think you are asking for a canter depart when you only wanted him to walk. On a young or uneducated horse, not trained to weight-shift cues, your weight shift could be very confusing. The horse is naturally going to try to stay underneath you so if you are off to one side he will adjust himself accordingly. But what if you did not want him to shift to the left or right? Now he is in trouble for adjusting to you when you did not even know you asked.

So you make a correction with your reins to fix the problem you are having in bringing the hindquarters across or turning for your next jump. The horse now as a conflict between coming under the weight or turning where you want him to go. What is he supposed to do? Ultimately in this situation, you are throwing your horse off balance and then forcing him to correct his balance in order to comply with your commands. Wouldn't it be easier if you sat straight and in the middle so that he did not have to make adjustments to begin with? I think your horse would gladly agree with this idea.

One more thing before we look at photos. You need to realize that horses have lateral balance issues also. Usually they bend easier in one direction than the other. If the horse bends better to the left his rib cage tends to remain expanded on the left side and shortened on the right side. In order to change the bend the horse needs to shift the rib cage so that it is longer on the right (outside of the bend). The strong hind leg results from the rib cage being slightly shifted toward that leg so that the push of the hind leg propels the horse's body forward. If the rib cage is not expanded on the outside the push from the outside hind leg travels across to the opposite shoulder. Therefore he falls on his left shoulder and is stiff to the left whereas he tends to fall in on the circle to the right. If we are going to train our horses to be balanced and equal on all four feet while going both directions then we have to help them become laterally balanced and supple. The idea of training the horse is to achieve this aim. With that in mind as we ride we need to think about what the finished product would be like. If we simply follow the horse's balance as it falls left or right then we will unconsciously lean and collapse through our body to comply with his.

If we are going to train horses to be straight then we need to carry ourselves as correctly as possible even when the horse is not. In this way we can influence the horse to achieve a better balance with less effort. This is similar to the idea of always playing tennis with someone better than you are so that you are always improving. If we let ourselves slop around on top of the horse there is no reason why he should try to improve his balance. He is simply going to deal with what we give him and be grateful when we finally get off his back. Instead, if we carry ourselves well then the horse has a greater chance of rising to the challenge of carrying himself. What this ultimately means is that instead of following the horse's imbalance we have to remain in balance in relation to gravity.

Here is what I mean. If the horse is falling in through the shoulder and the saddle is falling with him, we need to sit vertically in relation to gravity rather than follow the saddle. Once the horse lifts through the shoulder and balances from behind, then the saddle will come level again. But if we go with the saddle there is no way we can bring the horse back into balance because everything is leaning off to one side. Hopefully you never get so far out of balance that you have to sit way off to the side of the saddle. However, in some cases I have told students to sit "two inches to the left" in order to remain in the middle until the horse corrects himself.

In order to help you evaluate this series of photos I am going to point out some things to look for. Start with the rider's feet. Are they even across or is one foot lower than the other? Then notice if the saddle is in the middle of the horse's back or if it has shifted off to one side. Is it dropped on the same side as the "long leg" of the rider or to the opposite side? Look at the rider's clothing and notice if there are wrinkles only on one side. That would indicate that the ribs are collapsed on that side. Then imagine a line across the shoulders. Is it horizontal or angled? How does that line compare with another imaginary line running horizontally through the hips? Finally, look to see if the rider's head is tipped to one side. If you were to draw a vertical line straight down through the middle of the horse would it bisect? If not then there will be more weight on one side of the horse's back than the other. These are just some indicators to look for when evaluating the lateral balance of any rider.

PHOTO 1

The first thing I notice with this rider is that her feet are not even across from each other. The right foot is clearly "lower" than the left foot. I might guess that her stirrups are not even but that is hard to tell without measuring. Let's assume that they are even. Now look at the cantle of the saddle. Notice that it has shifted off to the left even though it is the right hind foot that is coming off the ground. Typically the saddle would appear

Photo 1

Photo 2

lower on the same side as the hind foot that is advancing. Also notice that this rider has a high left shoulder and a right shoulder that has dropped down and forward. In this picture a collapse is not so evident but I would guess that her right side is shorter than her left and she tends to push down on her right foot. To improve this picture I would first like to check and make sure the stirrups are even. Then I would straighten the saddle so that it is sitting in the middle of the horse's back. Finally I would have this rider think about breathing into the right side of her rib cage to expand the ribs and lengthen that side.

PHOTO 2

This rider has a very distinct collapse on the left side of her rib cage. (Typically women seem to collapse on the left and men on the right.) Notice how this rider is bracing against her stirrups, which is pushing her lower leg away from the horse. There is no

support for the horse when her leg is in this position. She is pushing harder into her left stirrup and, combined with her shortened left side, she has thrown her weight over to the right side of the horse's back. Notice that the saddle has been pushed to the right. As a result her entire right side is stretched. The tilt of the shoulders counterbalances the weight shifting outward through the lower body. This rider needs to soften at the back of the knees and bring her lower leg underneath her. That will eliminate the bracing so that she can even out the weight distribution across her seat. She needs to think about "shifting some sand" from her right leg across her pelvis into her left leg. That will help even her out from the waist down. Then opening up the ribs on the left will help to stabilize her weight across the seat. However, unless she quits bracing into her stirrups and softens her lower back there will be very little that will help this situation because she will go right back to pushing

Photo 3

Photo 4

harder with the left leg and sending her weight to the right.

PHOTO 3

My first comment about this combination is that the rider is not suitable for this horse. I would guess (as evidenced by what appears to be a therapeutic pad under the saddle) that this horse has back problems due to the weight of the rider. While I am not opposed to adults riding ponies and small horses, I do think it is important to consider the weight of the rider in relation to the constitution of the horse and the conformation of the horse's back. In any case it is obvious that this rider is sitting off to the right. He is fairly level across the feet and knees but the collapse on the left side of his back is placing more weight on the right seat bone. His left shoulder is dropped confirming that that side of the torso is shorter than the right. If he were to lengthen on the left side of his rib cage it would distribute his weight more

evenly across the saddle. Also by lengthening through the back he could better help this horse to carry his weight.

PHOTO 4

This rider looks fairly level across the shoulders. One large wrinkle is visible across the left side of the back of her shirt, which does not extend to the midline. If you consider the distance from the top of her hip to her underarm she looks fairly even. Now, draw an imaginary line through the middle of the horse's tail and see if it runs through the middle of her body. Notice that everything is tilted off to the left. Also notice that her right leg turns out at a different angle than her left leg. Angling her body will cause the right leg to brace away from the horse to counterbalance the left tilt. And as seen in so many riders who ride one-handed (see Photos 1, 2, 4, and 5), the shoulder of the hand holding the rein has a tendency to drop forward and down. This will create a twist in the torso, which can throw the rider's weight off to one side.

PHOTO 5

With this last rider, think of drawing a vertical straight line from the horse's tail through the top of his hat. Notice that the line would bisect the cantle of the saddle, line up with the seam on his jeans, and follow up through the middle of his hat. There are a few wrinkles on the right side and the shoulder line is not perfectly even. However, this rider is basically sitting evenly in the saddle with his weight distributed equally across both seat bones. The right leg does appear to be shorter than the left leg and there is a bit of a forward roll to the shoulders. I would suggest that this rider lengthen through the right rib cage by thinking of this side expanding as he breathes. The short right side (most likely

his dominant side) demonstrates that a contraction in the right side of the back will affect both shoulders and legs. The extremities close towards each other because the ribs have shifted away. By shifting the rib cage to the middle, the muscles of the shoulder and leg will relax lengthening that entire side.

If you don't have the opportunity to watch yourself in a mirror, have someone photograph or video you while you are riding. Look to see if your two sides are even. Even if you don't have access to these tools, notice how you are sitting on your horse the next time you ride. Do you feel more weight in one stirrup? Is there more weight on one seat bone? Do your ribs bulge out to one side? Is it the same as your horse? Then consciously think about making the distance from your hip to your shoulders equal and level. Notice what your horse does in response. Even if you think you are already level, experiment with different body postures and find out what happens. That way the next time your horse leans in on the turn you can correct your position and help him come back underneath you.

Photo 5

Two Thumbs Up

MORE THAN A POPULAR STATEMENT BY AMERICAN MOVIE critics, carrying your hands with the thumbs up significantly improves the transmission of information from you to your horse.

Most instructors will tell students to ride with the thumbnails pointing towards the sky, rather than toward each other in the classic "piano hands" position. However, without fully understanding the reasons behind this position and the muscular

This rider has good alignment of the elbow, wrist, and hand. Notice the straight line from the elbow to the reins. The hands are shoulder-width apart, thumbs on top, and the elbows are close to the torso.

This is what I call flat or "piano" hands. The thumbs point toward each other. The following movement in the arms and shoulders is restricted so the horse could easily get bumped in the mouth and restricted in the neck.

requirements to maintain it, most students quickly forget and allow their thumbs to sink down. Whether you are a beginner or advanced rider, conscious awareness of your hand position can serve as a diagnostic tool for stiffness and weakness in your body which directly affects your horse's performance.

Incorrect hand position is generally a symptom of a larger issue. Rather than being the cause of poor rider effectiveness, incorrect hand position can indicate a lack of fitness in the internal muscles of the torso and suppleness in the joints that is required for good riding. Beginner riders generally do not have the degree of body coordination and internal muscle strength necessary to maintain the correct riding position in motion. Beginners attempt to use gripping legs and upper body strength from shoulders, arms, and hands to try to stay on the horse rather than balance.

Beginners often take on some degree of the "fetal" or "protect your gut" position with pinching knees, drawn-up thighs, and clutching abdomen. The thumbs are naturally drawn down and together and the shoulders curl inward as part of that survival posture. This reflex is a statement of our strongest instinct—to grasp or hold on.

Overcoming survival posture is actually the greatest challenge riders face in order to attain unity and harmony with the horse. The reaction of holding on can be as subtle as inappropriately tightening a single muscle, which blocks the horse's movement. Most often when the rider "lets go" the horse releases the muscular contraction within his own body and goes forward in greater movement.

Once a rider has achieved some degree of body control and balance, the hand position can indicate the more subtle muscular issues. The cause for downward rotation of the thumbs often stems from weakness in the supporting muscles of the abdomen and back. Tension from work, school, or simply daily living is often carried in the upper body noted by tightness across the collarbones, shallow breathing, and a rounding of the shoulders. Unless a conscious effort is made to correct this tension on and off the horse, it will be carried over into riding. Uncorrected, the rider will habitually react first with the shoulder girdle rather than the

Here the wrists are cocked out. Notice the tension particularly on the inside (right wrist). The elbows are coming away from the rider's sides.

When the rider's hands are not level, the reins are at two different heights. This will transmit down the reins to the bit, which will no longer be level in the horse's mouth. This will cause a horse to tilt his head in response to the unlevel position of the bit.

This time the wrists are cocked inward, bringing the elbows too close to the body. A following movement of the arm will be restricted. Notice that the thumbs are now turning out. There is no longer a straight line through the arm to the reins. This will cause the rider to lean forward throwing her weight onto the horse's shoulders.

When the torso fails to support the rider, the arm and shoulder muscles automatically engage and the hips tighten in an unconscious reaction to stay on the horse. While riders may find strength in their shoulders to resist a pulling horse, they will have to lock joints which prohibits movement, use tremendous muscular effort in the upper body, and increase overall body stiffness to get the horse to respond. Riders in self-carriage—those who have developed the strength and coordination of the torso for balance and support—can be fluid in their limbs and subtle with their aids.

The Spanish Riding School in Vienna serves as a model for rider self-carriage. There you will see fluidly elegant riders sitting in self-carriage without tension thus allowing and receiving the movement of the horse.

In order to switch from instinctively hanging on the reins to conscious self-carriage, riders need to develop awareness of their hands and the instinctive position changes that occur in reaction to a loss of balance either in themselves or their horses. Then

seat and back for strength and support. The rider's seat will be disengaged from the hands until the rider begins to use the torso for support and release the ball and socket joint of the shoulders.

The muscles of the torso are the foundation muscles for riding in balance without gripping, initiating correct half-halts.

new neuromuscular patterns can be developed by consciously using the internal muscles of the torso and correcting the hand position to respond instead of tightening the shoulders, arms, and hands. The ring of muscles in the torso, the abdomen, and back are the muscles activated in a correct half-halt and by Sally Swift's directive to "Center and Grow."

To re-pattern the habitual reaction of grasping the reins, the rider must become aware and then inhibit the reaction of pulling back. The hands then become telegraph lines relaying information to the body. Then torso muscles can be used to reestablish the horse's balance. Using only the torso may be sufficient to achieve the desired result. If not, hand and leg aids can be used in conjunction with the torso as a response, not a reaction, to the horse. Subtle responsive rein and leg aids result from fine motor control skills which are present only when the grasping gross motor reflex of hanging on is gone. This entire process requires that the rider override the instinct to grab and hang on in response to a pull. Remember the horse's strongest reflex is flight.

Combine a highly flight-oriented horse with a rider that simply reacts instinctively by grabbing, and you have a recipe for disaster. When the rider is in self-carriage the only action is taken in response to the horse's movement, never in reaction. Many times the action taken is simply to sustain balance of self in order to allow the horse to find his own balance. While this sounds simple, waiting for the horse can take tremendous strength in the back and abdomen. Over-correction by the rider can easily throw the horse off balance in yet another direction so timing and coordination with the horse's movement are important.

All this seems to be a long way from thumbs up. Yet the answer to the problem of hand position lies not just in the hands

themselves but in training the torso to sustain the rider in self-carriage. Observing hand position provides information to both rider and instructor regarding the rider's body use.

Exercises to develop biceps and triceps are therefore inappropriate because the weakness is not in the upper body but in the torso. Just as the horse needs to develop the proper muscles for correct work, so too must the rider. If the rider needs tremendous upper body strength to hold the horse then neither horse nor rider is in self-carriage. Emphasis needs to be placed in releasing the shoulders and establishing a connection from the hands to the rider's back.

A conscious effort to hold the hands with the thumbs in the correct position, pointing upward, will start making changes throughout the rider's entire body and begin developing the connection between the seat and hands. By carrying the hands correctly, the torso will engage and become stronger because the rider cannot rely on the shoulders for strength.

By consciously developing these new habitual patterns, riders can recognize when the horse is off balance and/or they have lost self-carriage because the thumbs will start to point sideways. Rather than locking and grasping to correct the horse's balance, the rider can open the shoulder, return the thumb to the upright position, and use seat and back to straighten and lighten the horse.

EXERCISES TO DEVELOP AWARENESS OF HANDS AND IMPROVE HAND POSITION

Start by shaking one hand allowing all the fingers to hang freely. Now tighten one finger. Notice what happens to your ability to shake your hand.

Sit in a chair and pretend to hold the

Riding with a short stick between your hands can help improve your hand position. Notice that thumbs are still on top and the stick is under the thumbs. The fingers are softly closed on the reins. Don't be surprised at first if this feels extremely awkward.

reins. Now look down at your hands and hold them correctly so that the thumbnails are pointing towards the sky while the pad of the thumb is in contact with the rein on top of the index finger. Move your arms back and forth in a "following" motion with the imaginary horse. Notice the freedom of movement in the entire shoulder girdle. Notice the elbows gliding forward and back past the rib cage. Now rotate the hands so that the thumbs point towards each other in a classic "piano" hands position and repeat the above movements. Notice now that the movement is less fluid, has a shorter range of motion, and creates tightness across the collarbones, biceps, elbows, and wrists. Exaggerate the two positions to really feel the difference. Then explore how little rotation is necessary to create tension.

Still sitting in a chair and continuing to hold your imaginary reins, tighten across the collarbones, drawing your shoulders inward. Observe the tendency of the hands to rotate and be drawn together. Now widen the collarbones apart without pulling the shoulders back. Notice that the hands

tend to widen and lighten allowing the elbow to glide back and forth.

Repeat these two exercises holding a rope or a pair of reins detached from a bridle. Have someone else hold the other ends and let them tell you what they feel as you explore tightening and releasing different parts of the shoulders, arms, and hands as well as different correct and incorrect hand positions. Let the other person give you feedback on what they feel as you make different changes.

When riding, place a crop or stick underneath your thumbs connecting your two hands and keeping them about six inches apart. Now ride and notice how much it "gets in the way" of your habitual hand position.

Observe whether the stick remains level at all times or if one end drops (indicating that your hands are not level). Notice, especially during transitions, whether you nearly break the stick as the thumbs attempt to rotate down and inward. (Careful, if your stick is not thick enough

When riding one handed you still want a basic straight line position from the elbow to the hand so that your arm and shoulder are free in order to follow the horse's head movement. The other arm hangs from the shoulder in such a way that you could simply swing the arm into place for two-handed riding.

and your unconscious habit of rotating your hands is strong enough, you may break it!) Notice what other parts of your body begin to work when you can no longer engage the hands and shoulder girdle to force the horse into balance.

Finally, an image to think about is carrying two ice cream cones, one in each hand. Everyone has seen how unhappy children become when they let their hands rotate and the ice cream winds up on the sidewalk. Remember to keep your thumbs up so that the ice cream does not fall off the imaginary cones.

Take a little time to become more aware of your hands and let them tell you what is going on in your body behind the scenes. Remember, good hands begin with releasing the shoulders and correctly using the torso for support, not the reins. Then the judge will give you two thumbs up and more importantly, your horse will too.

PART THREE

TIMING

Knowing When to Ask

*I*N ORDER TO INFLUENCE THE HORSE WITH A MINIMUM OF EFFORT IT IS important to time your aids correctly. With this in mind, I am going to define aids as anything you would use to create or inhibit movement in the horse: seat, legs, feet, hands, voice, whip, spur, stick, rope, and/or mecate. If your timing is accurate and consistent, it will require a minimum amount of effort with your aids to make a change in the horse. If your timing is off, you will have to resort to much greater strength and effort to get the horse to do what you want.

As the horse gains understanding, your aids can be reduced to a

minimum. In the beginning it is helpful to combine aids to make your request clear—seat, legs, and hands may all need to act together. As the horse learns the meaning of the aids the requests can be reduced to just the seat, provided that it was correctly employed in the first place. In other words, when asking for a canter depart from a green horse the rider would make the request very clear by using seat, legs, and maybe even a stick or mecate. Once the horse understands, the canter aid can be just the seat. To understand the concept of using a minimum of aids, consider a closed door. You can pound, kick, shove, and beat on the door all day long (if it is a strong one). Or you can turn the doorknob releasing the latch and open it without any effort. This is a lot like trying to influence horses. You can use brute force against horses and eventually get them to do what you want, or you can ask quietly at the right moment in the right location on their body to produce the desired effect.

Ultimately, getting the horse to move in the desired way has a lot to do with physics and geometry. These are included in the science of biomechanics. I know, you barely survived chemistry so why am I bringing up physics? Because physics dictates a lot of what happens with the horse. Once again we come back to gravity. Gravity (a physical principle) acts on all objects on this earth all the time. Gravity is what keeps us on the horse. Without gravity, as I've mentioned before, we would simply float away. The horse is also influenced by gravity. Therefore, if we want to use a minimum of effort to influence the horse's feet, it helps to understand some basic physics. That way we can ask at the moment when the horse can respond by moving the desired leg.

For example, if you want the horse to pick up his right front foot, the horse cannot be bearing weight on that foot. If he is, he is going to have to shift the weight off that foot

Walk: A four-beat gait where each foot moves separately.

Trot: A two-beat gait where the feet move in diagonal pairs.

Canter: A three-beat gait where one hind foot lands first, then the other hind and its diagonal front foot, then the remaining front foot.

before lifting it, otherwise gravity is going to make it impossible for the horse to move that foot. For those of you who need to feel

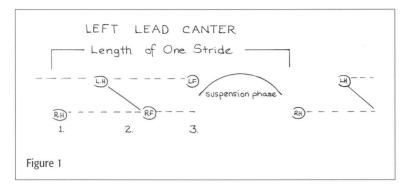

LEFT LEAD CANTER

Length of One Stride

suspension phase

1.   2.   3.

Figure 1

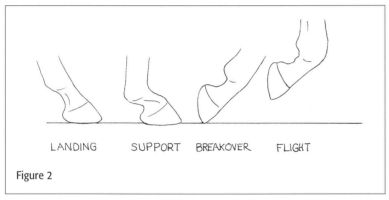

LANDING   SUPPORT   BREAKOVER   FLIGHT

Figure 2

horse has completed one stride. The *stride length* is determined by measuring the distance covered by one stride (Fig. 1). For example, in left-lead canter, you could measure the distance from the right hind hoofprint to right hind hoofprint following one cycle of movement. It helps to have a freshly dragged arena for this measurement.

The *gait* is a pattern of footfalls. (See photos on page 87.) The walk is a four-beat gait in which each foot moves separately. If you were to listen to the walk you would hear four-beats/stride since there is a sound for each foot. The trot is a two-beat gait. The legs move in diagonal pairs so you only hear two-beats/stride. The canter is a three-beat gait (like a waltz) so you would hear three-beats/stride. The pace is a two-beat gait like the trot except that lateral pairs of legs (legs on the same side) are moving at the same time. The so-called "soft-gaited" horses such as Tennessee Walkers and Missouri Fox Trotters have a variety of footfall patterns. Since I am not an expert on the soft gaits, I will restrict my discussion to the three basic gaits of walk, trot, and canter.

In order to find the timing of your aids it is helpful to understand the different phases of the leg movement. I will describe the flight pattern of the limb as four different phases: landing, support, breakover, and flight (Fig. 2). Landing is when the hoof contacts the ground. Support is when the horse's weight is over the limb. Breakover is the moment when the foot is leaving the ground. Flight is the phase where the limb is traveling through the air. Each leg goes through these four phases as the horse moves. For that matter so do your legs when you move!

In a sound horse the flight pattern of each limb will be rhythmic, even, flowing, and synchronized. The hoof hits the ground

this, do the following exercise. Stand up and shift your weight onto your right foot. Now try to walk forward starting with your right leg. You can't unless you first shift your weight to the left leg. So if you know where the horse's weight is at any given moment you can position the horse before you ask for something so that the horse can respond correctly. If the horse is not in that position, you need to shift the balance first, then ask, and then the horse can respond with the desired movement.

At this point I am sure you are nodding your head in agreement. The next question is "when is the right time to ask so that it takes a minimum of effort?" First we need to examine how the horse moves (locomotion) so we know when to ask. Let's start with some terminology. A *stride* is when the horse has moved all four feet in a series. The legs go through a cycle of movement. When all four feet have gone through one cycle the in the landing phase. As the horse moves forward his body weight comes over the leg. (Think of a pole vaulter at the top of the vault. His weight is directly over the pole.) The leg forms a column of support for the weight. The leg will coil or compress in landing and support phases. Then at the end of support the elastic recoil will spring the leg forward in the propulsion phase of the stride. It is best if this propulsive force occurs while the hoof is still under the body. If propulsion happens after the body has passed over the leg, the angle of propulsion will be forward and down instead of forward and up causing the horse to fall onto the forehand. In breakover the horse begins to lift the toe off the ground immediately after the push. Finally, the flight phase is when the leg is in the air round in appearance. Each joint moves fluidly.

When a horse is unlevel or lame, the visual appearance of the leg movement is altered. The sequence and symmetry of the limb phases are disturbed. There will be a lack of flow when observing the horse move. If you count the footfalls or listen to the footfalls there will be a distinct arrhythmia to the sound. The stride length may be reduced. One or more legs will look out of sync with the other legs. The visual appearance will depend on the severity of the problem. There might be just a minor hesitation to the limb movement or a major limp.

To get an idea of visual alterations in the different phases of the stride in the lame horse, think of the following scenarios. A horse that has an abscess is an example of supporting phase lameness. The horse will not want to bear weight on that foot. The support phase on that limb will be reduced. The horse will try to keep as much weight as possible off that leg when it does come into support. Depending on the severity of a front foot abscess, the horse will lift the

head and neck dramatically to unload the abscessing foot.

Shoulder and stifle lameness can cause a visual change in the breakover phase. If there is a problem flexing the elbow or stifle, breakover will become longer. The horse will look like he is dragging his toes. Lack of joint flexibility can be visible in flight phase. If the horse is sore in the hocks the leg will look stiff, straight-legged, or short in the flight phase. In the landing phase notice if the toe stabs into the ground. This can result from poor shoeing or joint problems. If the horse is landing toe first dirt will fly up in front of the toe rather than at the heel.

In addition to the legs, the rib cage of the horse also moves. Rib cage movement has a lot to do with the feeling of swing in the horse's back. The rib cage can move side to side, up and down, and diagonally. An upward swinging rib cage enables the hind legs to step deeply underneath the horse. A stiff rib cage will inhibit the hind leg from coming under. If there is too much sideways swing the horse may not be using his back properly to carry weight. It is important to recognize not enough vs. too much swing in the rib cage.

When a horse bends his body he moves the rib cage so that the body appears to be curved. (Flexing the neck does not necessarily create bend in the body although it is commonly used to create bend.) When the horse bends correctly, the rib cage shifts so that the sternum moves slightly up and away from the bend. The ribs will expand slightly on the outside of the curve and contract slightly on the inside. The withers will remain vertical. If the withers are tilting away from the desired bend then the horse may not actually be bending. Instead he may be leaning or the rib cage may be bulging into the bend.

Most of the bending in the horse occurs just behind the withers. The neck reflects the

Here, my horse Andy standing relaxed and relatively straight.

When I lift Andy's back up, the rib cage area fills behind the withers. This lifting occurs when the horse uses his back correctly under saddle.

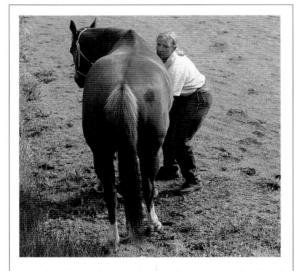

I am bending Andy to the left. Notice that the right side of his rib cage has lifted and expanded while the left side of his rib cage has shortened. His head and neck follow the bend of the thoracic spine (rib cage area). Andy has lifted his back as he bends.

Here, Andy is bending to the right. Notice that this is not as clear a bend as to the left. Andy has leaned a little to the left in addition to bending right. However, he is still lifting through his back and his rib cage is more expanded on the outside of the bend while closing on the inside.

bend. There is little movement sideways in the lower part of the spine. Therefore, the bending curve is not continuous from front to back, as you can see in these photos of Andy. It is important that the horse lifts the back as he bends. As a result of the lift and

bend the back muscles on the outside of the bend will appear to rise up while the inside will dip a little. As the horse comes into a higher degree of collection the amount of side-to-side swing will decrease because there is more upward lift of the rib cage. The lift of the back provides room for the pelvis to come further under the horse and rider.

When the rib cage is stiff the horse will be rigid. Responsiveness to aids greatly decreases. The horse will be difficult to move forward or bend. Remember, when the rib cage is rigid the hind leg can't easily swing under. In extreme cases, horses that are braced in inhalation can be explosive, responding by bucking and rearing because they can't soften their rib cage to move forward.

To understand this concept, think of when someone poked you in the ribs. Typically, especially if you are ticklish, you collapsed where you were prodded. Your ribs gave way under the pressure. But what if you wanted to prove that you weren't ticklish? You did your weight-lifter impersonation by taking a deep breath and holding it. This made your rib cage rigid so you could withstand your annoying friend. (By the way, the nerves that respond to tickling are the same nerves that register pain.) To

feel what this is like do your body builder impression and take a really deep breath. Hold it and walk around. What happens to your movement? Notice how stiff your turning and bending becomes when you hold your breath.

The opposite of a rigid rib cage is one that swings too much. The abdominal muscles have a lot to do with supporting internal organ weight the horse. When the abdominal muscles are flabby the back and rib cage can sag down giving the appearance of a hay belly. Notice on older brood mares that their entire midsection looks like it has fallen. Without good muscle tone it will be difficult to lift the back (Fig. 3, left). As these saggy horses move there is a lot of side-to-side swing through the middle of their body. The inability to raise the midsection will diminish forward motion. The push from the hind leg dissipates through the midsection rather then propelling the entire body forward. Adding weight onto a horse in this posture worsens this condition unless the rider really supports the horse through the seat (Fig. 3, right).

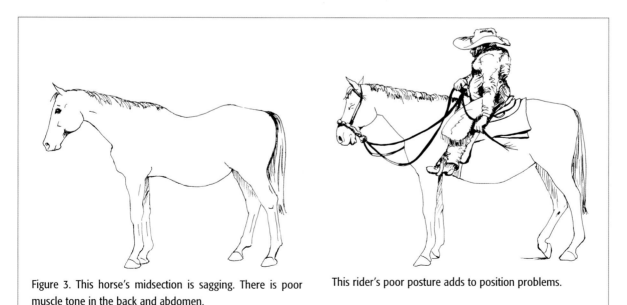

Figure 3. This horse's midsection is sagging. There is poor muscle tone in the back and abdomen.

This rider's poor posture adds to position problems.

To understand the effect of too much sideways swing in the rib cage, think of sitting on your mother's dining room chairs. If you rock side to side eventually you will weaken the braces and the legs will spread apart. Ultimately you will break the chair. But if you slide your seat forward on the chair it will not be damaged. The joints of the chair cannot withstand the sideways movement. Neither can the horse's limbs. Eventually the horse will show signs of wear in the joints and back if there is too much sideways swing. More importantly, you will lose forward motion since the back is no longer functioning as a bridge between the hindquarters and the forehand. When the horse works through the back, he creates forward motion in the rider's seat.

By understanding how the horse functions biomechanically the rider can influence the movement of the legs and rib cage. Encouraging the correct movement will decrease stress on the joints (and the mind) of the horse because he will be able to carry the rider's weight more efficiently with less effort. If the horse is not using himself well it also will be harder to make quick stops, starts, and turns.

\\\

Feeling the Walk

*T*O RECAP FROM THE LAST CHAPTER, A STRIDE IS WHEN ALL FOUR legs have moved through one cycle. Walk is a four-beat, trot is a two-beat, and canter is a three-beat pattern of leg movement called a gait. Stride length is the distance covered when one cycle of leg movement has been completed. For purposes of discussion, the movement of each limb has been divided into four phases: landing, support, breakover, and flight. The rib cage also needs to move. The direction of the rib cage can be up and down,

Place the back of your hand on your lower back to feel the movement of the back moving towards the horse's tail at the walk.

side to side, and diagonal. Swing in the rib cage allows the hind legs to step underneath the horse's body.

In order to influence the horse with the least amount of effort (minimal aids) a rider needs to time the aids *within* the movement of the horse. This will create a continuous flow rather than abruptly interrupting the horse to make a correction and then starting again. Interrupting the horse may be necessary at times, especially with a green horse. However, by timing the aids within the movement, the rider's aids will become more subtle, requiring less effort. The mes-

sage to the horse will be much clearer with less delay allowing for concise communication, or harmony, between horse and rider. In order to time the aids within the movement, the rider needs to know when the horse is going through the different phases of the stride.

So how does the rider know when each leg is moving and what phase of the stride the horse is in? There are landmarks that the rider can look and feel for during each of the different phases. Once the rider can identify the different phases it will be much easier to correctly time the aids for various movements. To feel the landmarks the rider needs to sit in a position that provides optimum balance and feel with minimum effort, a neutral position. To establish this neutral position the seat bones need to point down towards the ground while sitting in the saddle (refer back to Part One on Alignment).

FIND YOUR SEAT

In order to find out if your seat bones are pointing down it might help if you place the back of one hand on your lower back at your belt line (while you are on your horse). Feel this part of your back and check that it is flat while you remain open across your

Figure 1. The rider's lower back is moving toward the horse's tail.

You want to place your hand at the level of your belt.

chest. As the horse walks the lower back will move toward the horse's tail each stride (Fig. 1). If the lower back is moving toward the horse's ears you are hollowing your back. This will point your seat bones behind you and decrease the amount of feeling you will have in your seat. If you are slumping in the saddle you will feel roundness in your back, your chest will cave in, and most likely your feet will be way out in front of you. In this case your seat bones will be rolled too far under. You will be sitting only on your buttock muscles.

If you are unsure which way your seat bones are pointing, go back to the exercise where you sit on your hands, either in the saddle or on a flat hard surface. Feel the change in position of your seat bones as you go from a rounded back position to an arched back position. Somewhere in between you will find your seat bones pointing down.

You might find you are a bit sore after this lesson. Don't worry. By engaging your hamstring and buttocks muscles your seat bones will have a muscle layer covering them to reduce the direct pressure. At first, decreasing the tone in your seat will let you know exactly where your seat bones are. If it is too uncomfortable engage your seat just enough to lift the seat bones slightly off the saddle but not completely.

ENGAGE YOUR SEAT

To feel engagement of your seat, again place your hands under your seat bones. Notice that by tightening the muscles on the bottom of your pelvis, buttocks, and hamstrings you can lift your seat bones off your hands. Go through the entire range of motion from seat bones totally resting on your hands (ouch!) to completely lifting them off (you will only feel the muscles). Find a middle place where you can still feel your seat bones but have some muscle

Feel the push up into your seat by placing your hands underneath your seat bones. (Have someone lead your horse if you do both hands at the same time.)

around them lifting them slightly, just enough to have both muscle and bone in contact with your hand. As long as you can feel your seat bones you will be able to do the following exercises.

For these exercises I suggest you use an experienced quiet horse that allows you the opportunity to explore the different movements without having to worry much about him. If you are in a contained environment like a round pen or can have someone who lead or longe you, you might try closing your eyes to enhance your sense of feel. If for any reason you are uncomfortable with your eyes closed then, please, open your eyes.

If you have chosen to close your eyes, once you have familiarized yourself with the feelings in the following exercises open your eyes and see if you can continue to feel the movements. Finally, take your reins and feel the movements while having to direct the horse. Begin to slowly exaggerate some of the movements described below and find out what happens. Does the horse increase his stride? Does he wobble more or less? Does he fall on the forehand, the shoulders, or shift back onto the hindquarters? Then minimize the movements and see how the horse responds. Ask yourself what effect your movement has on his movement. By exploring and understanding all the different possibilities in a quiet relaxed manner you will understand how to create and combine different feelings for the specific movements you want to do later on (e.g., transitions and lateral work).

WORKING AT THE WALK

As described earlier, the walk is a four-beat gait. To time your aids properly you will want to be able to distinguish each foot during the walk. In addition there are ways to distinguish the different phases of the stride: landing, support, breakover, and flight.

If you are walking on a hard surface, listen to the sound of the four feet as they strike the ground. This is the landing phase of the stride (when the foot strikes the ground). Count the sound to yourself. Does the walk have a steady rhythm or is there a long pause between two of the feet? In other words, is one beat accented such as "1, **2**, 3, 4; 1, **2**, 3, 4; 1, **2**, 3, 4" or even "1, 2, 3, 4, 1, 2, 3, 4"? Make sure you aren't just getting into your own desired rhythm instead of listening to the horse (you would be surprised how often this happens).

Change the speed of the walk and listen to how the sounds of the footfalls alter. Do they get more or less regular as you increase or decrease the speed of the walk? What happens to the sounds when you walk a circle? When there is a quick leg or a delayed leg it means the horse is not reaching equally on all four legs. When the sound is consistently even, rhythmic, and steady like a metronome (an instrument that marks time by ticking) then the horse has a good walk.

Next notice your seat bones. The seat bones will tell you when the support, breakover, and flight phases occur in the hind legs. During support you will feel an upward push into your seat bones. In flight you will feel a forward movement with a

slight dip. Breakover is at the change from the push to the dip feeling. Within this cycle of movement the horse can move your seat bones in three possible directions. Depending on the quality of the walk you will feel one direction more clearly than another. The three directions are forward and back, side-to-side, and up and down.

The side-to-side movement is the least useful of the three directions. If the horse is throwing your seat bones sideways then he is not using his back correctly to carry the weight of the rider. This is a difficult fault to correct in the walk. The walk does not have any suspension (moment when all four feet are off the ground at the same time) so if the movement is primarily lateral (sideways), the horse is swinging the rib cage left and right like a pendulum to step the hind legs under. The "bridge" (midsection of the body) at this point is disconnected from the two ends. In other words, you have an engine (hindquarters) but no transmission (midsection) to send the power from the back end to the front end. Therefore you will not have very much "energy" or forward push from the hind legs propelling the body forward when you ask for a larger walk. All you will get is more swing through the middle. You may feel like you are sitting in a hole on this kind of horse with your seat bones primarily swinging left and right. A walk of this kind may appear "busy" (lots of feet moving) but in fact covers very little ground since there is no transmission of energy through the midsection.

The opposite of the dippy-backed horse with the swinging rib cage is the horse about to buck. A bucking horse has rounded up the midsection of his body as much as possible. The rider will feel no movement in the seat bones sideways, forward, or back, only up. The midsection has expanded and stiffened the rib cage so that other directions of movement cannot occur.

While you don't want this much "up" in your seat, you do want to feel that kind of lift increase under your direction during the walk. This "up" feeling should increase as you collect the horse. If you do not get increased lift in the back then you do not have true collection. As the horse lifts the back he stabilizes the midsection so that the power from the hindquarters is transmitted to the front end lifting the rider and the shoulders. Notice that if your horse is moving correctly with his back up you will feel predominantly the forward-back motion in your seat bones with a minimum of side-to-side motion.

CLOSE YOUR EYES

Let's go back to walking with your eyes closed. Notice the forward-back motion in your seat bones. Can you feel both seat bones? Are they moving in the same direction (i.e., is one going more sideways, has less upward lift, or is nonexistent)? Is the forward-back movement more prominent than the side-to-side movement? If not, inhibit the side-to-side and gently encourage the forward-back movement. Does the horse walk out more?

Decrease the forward-back movement. Does your horse slow down? Can you stop your horse without using your reins by decreasing the amount of forward-back movement in your seat? Check to make sure you did not switch to side-to-side in the halt indicating that the horse dropped his back and "stalled" into the halt. When the horse is working through the back you will be able to increase and decrease the forward motion by increasing and decreasing the amount of forward-back movement in your seat bones.

On a straight line notice if the forward-back movement of your seat is equal on the two sides. If not the horse may be stepping short with one hind leg. In other words the horse will not be going straight unless the feeling from behind is equal. When walking

on a circle what happens to the forward-back motion? You might notice that the outside seat bone feels like it is traveling farther than the inside one. The inside seat bone may feel like it is moving more vertically. This is because the outside seat bone has a farther distance to travel on a curve than the inside due to the circumference of the circle being different on the two sides of the horse.

Now look for the support phase of the hind legs. Start with one side, then the other, then both hind legs, alternating left, right. To begin bring your awareness to your left seat bone. Feel how the horse lifts and drops that seat bone. If you are having a difficult time feeling the lift (perhaps because the horse is not pushing strongly off that hind leg) place your hand on the point of the horse's hip on the left side (Fig. 2). Straighten out your elbow so that your upper body weight is resting on your hand. Feel the upward push of the iliac crest (point of the hip) in your hand. Now put your hand under your left buttock. Feel the push up into your seat from the horse. This is the support phase of the left

Figure 2. Feel the push from the hind foot by placing your hand on the point of the horse's hip.

hind leg in walk. Feel this movement in your seat without having to sit on your hand.

NOTICE THE RHYTHM

Say the word "now" out loud when you feel the push from the hind leg. By verbalizing the feeling you are using both sides of your brain. It also gives you feedback about how fast you can feel and respond. Responding to the feeling (timing your aids) will be important when you actually want to do something about the horse's stride. Verbalizing will help you process the information you are receiving from the horse. The right brain is feeling the movement while the left side is involved with verbalizing the feeling. You can hear yourself count out the stride. Sometimes it is difficult to say the feeling as it is happening. By practicing this skill you will rapidly improve your timing because you are incorporating both sides of your brain.

Repeat the exercise, feeling for the support phase of the right hind leg. If there are others in the arena with you, watch their horses and see how their hips are pushed forward and upward as the horse pushes off the ground in the support phase of the hind legs. Watch each other and listen to see if you have the verbal "now" happening at the moment when the horse is pushing with the appropriate hind leg. Once you have identified the support phase on each hind leg separately, verbalize both hind legs by alternating "left, right, left, right" during the support phase of each hind leg.

Listen and feel the rhythm of the two hind feet. Ask yourself the following questions: Do you feel an equal amount of push from each hind leg? Is the push consistent? If you feel one stronger than the other, which leg is it? If you are having a hard time identifying what you are feeling and you happen to have an arena mirror, watch yourself as you walk by and match up the feeling with the visual picture in the mirror.

If you don't have a mirror you can always use the shadows on the ground. Be careful not to tip to one side in order to watch the shadow. Or if you are lucky enough to have a riding buddy, ask him or her to call out the different phases so you can feel the moments when they occur.

Next feel for the flight phase of the hind limbs at walk. If the lift up in your seat is the support phase, then the dip in your seat is the flight phase. Feel the "dip, dip, dip, dip" left and right. Again, verbalize the feelings. Use your hands by placing them on the top of the pelvis (yours and/or the horse's) if you need help. Once you have identified the support and flight phase of the stride, breakover should be pretty easy. Remember, breakover is that brief moment after the push and before the dip. This is a very brief moment so you may not actually feel the breakover. However you will know when it happens because it comes between the supporting (push) and flight (dip) feelings. Landing is at the end of the dip. You can identify landing by the sound of the hoof hitting the ground.

WRAPPING UP THE WALK

Now you are able to feel and identify all four phases of the hind legs at the walk: the sound of the striking hoof in landing, the push into each seat bone for the support phase, the dip in the seat bone for flight phase, and the brief moment between push and dip for breakover. You will be able to influence the stride of the horse through your seat by either increasing or decreasing the amount of glide in your seat bones which will increase or decrease the stride length. You might even be able to halt your horse without using the reins by decreasing the movement in your seat until it is so small the horse halts. It is important in this exercise that you do not "lock up" your seat otherwise the horse will stall into the halt.

20

Timing the Aids in the Walk

L ET'S RECAP WHAT WE HAVE SO FAR AND THEN CONTINUE TO FIND the timing in the walk.

Aids are anything we can use to influence the horse's movement. For the purposes of this discussion we are look-

ing at the natural aids—seat, legs, and hands—to influence the horse. Good timing of the aids allows us to influence the horse with a minimum of effort. In order to use a minimum of effort we need to time our aids within the movement of the horse. When

the aids are applied correctly we can change the horse's stride length, speed, foot placement, and degree of collection with very subtle cues.

It is important to time the aids within the movement so that we do not unnecessarily disrupt the horse. This will allow the horse time to think, understand, and learn what we are asking. If our aids are badly timed the horse will have greater difficulty understanding our requests. The results will be what we asked for but that may not have been what we wanted.

TIME THE AIDS

To time the aids within the horse's movement we need to know what is moving when. Each leg goes through a cycle, which can be broken down into four phases: landing, support, breakover, and flight. There are landmarks to feel each of these phases. By knowing when the horse is moving through the different phases the rider can apply aids at the right time to alter the movement at the moment when the horse is most capable of responding.

The rider can best feel the movement of the horse by riding in a basic balanced position. This position requires that the rider's seat bones point down. When the seat bones point down the rider has skeletal support. A basic balanced position enables us to have less tension in the legs while remaining in balance with the horse's movement. Less tension in the rider's legs means that there will be greater freedom and more independence to apply the required aids without affecting other parts of the body. This position also gives the rider the greatest amount of "feel" through the seat.

It is the movement created by the horse in the rider's body, particularly the seat and legs, that tells the rider what the horse is doing. It is the ability of the rider to control the movement in her back, seat, and legs

that influences the horse to change his movement (i.e., transitions, turns, increase/decrease stride) thereby allowing the rider to let go of the reins.

THE WALK

The walk is a four-beat gait. Each foot strikes the ground individually. There should be three feet on the ground at all times during the stride. This means that there is no suspension (time when all the feet are off the ground) in the walk. A good walk is rhythmic and forward with a good length of stride. The hind feet reach deeply underneath the body of the horse in order to provide impulsion. The rider can determine the different phases of the stride at the walk by the feelings in the seat. The rider can also influence the stride at the walk using the different aids at the right time in the stride.

The movement received by the rider's seat bones tells the rider what the hind feet are doing. The horse can move the rider's seat in three possible directions: forward-back, side-side, and up-down. Side to side, we learned in the last chapter, is the least useful direction. Too much side to side and the horse is not using his back correctly. Not enough, however, and you have a laterally stiff horse (no bend). Forward-back is the direction that we want to go. A strong forward-back feel means the horse is working through the back and moving well forward. The up-down feeling is created by the push of the horse's hind feet. Knowing when this occurs can tell us when each leg is going through the different phases of the stride.

We ended the last chapter with the rider being able to feel the different phases of the stride in the hind legs. When the rider feels a lift in a seat bone the horse is in support phase on that hind limb (the horse is pushing off the ground with that hind foot). The "dip" feeling in the seat is the flight phase. The moment between the push and the dip is the breakover of that hind foot. You can hear the landing phase if you are walking on a hard surface. It is just after the dip and before the push. By feeling the two hind feet and then decreasing or encouraging the movement through the seat, the rider can increase or decrease the stride length and speed. It is important not to dissociate the seat from the legs when you do this. If you dissociate the seat, then all you are doing is wobbling your pelvis and not influencing the horse. When you use your seat correctly there is a sense of firmness and immediate response by the horse. If the horse is not responding to a subtle increase in the seat movement then the legs, a stick, or the lead of your mecate rein can be used to keep the horse light and listening.

FEELING THE FEET

To continue, we need to find the different phases of the stride for the front feet. Begin again by placing your pelvis in a neutral position. Make sure your legs are hanging down underneath your seat. Pushing your feet out in front of you will block the movement of the horse. The rigidity in your leg will also make it difficult to find the movement of the front legs in your body.

Again, remember that these lessons are designed to be done on a quiet horse in a safe environment allowing you time to explore what you're doing in relation to the horse. Performing some of the following exercises with your eyes closed will enhance your sense of feel but if for any reason you are uncomfortable with your eyes closed then open your eyes. It is also helpful to have a ground person who can assist you in discovering the relationship between you and your horse's body. The ground person can call out the different phases so that you can match a feeling to her voice. Conversely, you can call out the different phases and they can check to see if you have it right.

The top of the shoulder blade has moved forward.

The top of the shoulder blade has moved back.

To feel the front legs start by looking down at the horse's left front shoulder. Notice that the shoulder blade moves forward (becomes more horizontal) (Fig. 1, left) and back (becomes more vertical) with each step (Fig. 1, right). When the front leg is traveling through the air (flight phase of the stride) the point of the shoulder travels towards the horse's nose. The top of the shoulder blade by the withers moves back and down towards the saddle. (Hence it is

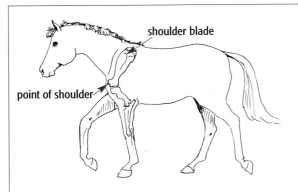
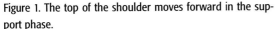
shoulder blade

point of shoulder

Figure 1. The top of the shoulder moves forward in the support phase.

The top of the shoulder moves back in the flight phase.

important to check saddle fit in motion. The shoulder blade can be pinched as the horse moves if the saddle does not fit properly.) When the leg is in the support phase of the stride the point of the shoulder is going back. As the horse advances over the limb the top of the shoulder blade becomes more vertical.

Now look at your knee and thigh in relation to the horse's shoulder. Notice that your thigh also moves forward/up and back/down with each stride. Therefore, your knee and thigh mirror the shoulder

blade of the horse provided your legs are not rigid. If you are having difficulty seeing this, place your hand on your thigh and feel how it is moving. Notice that your thighs alternate in the movement just as the horse's shoulders alternate. As one shoulder is going forward the other is going back. Pay attention to the moment when your knee changes from the back/down movement to the forward/up movement. That is the moment of breakover for that front foot. Landing phase would be the opposite—when the knee changes from the forward/up to the back/down motion.

This rider has his foot pushed out in front blocking the movement in the thigh. Therefore he will not be able to feel the movement of the shoulder in his knee and thigh.

The rider's thigh follows the movement of the horse's shoulder.

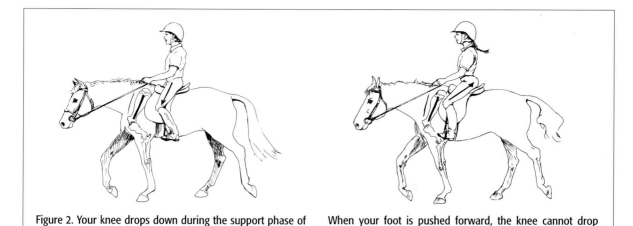

Figure 2. Your knee drops down during the support phase of the front leg.

When your foot is pushed forward, the knee cannot drop down. Therefore the thigh pushes up into the hip.

Count out the rhythm of the two front feet just as we did for the hind feet. Notice whether the count is even and rhythmical. Walk on a hard surface if necessary to hear the landing of the front feet. Close your eyes and feel the motion of the front feet corresponding to your thighs. As an experiment push your legs out in front of you stiffening your knees, and find out what happens to the feeling. Notice that when the leg stiffens the thigh no longer drops down during the support phase (Fig. 2, right). Instead, the thigh pushes back and up into the hip socket affecting the contact of your seat with the saddle. You will in effect push yourself out of the saddle instead of letting your seat deepen into the saddle.

WHAT GETS IN YOUR WAY?

Pushing on your stirrups (which is different from having your heel down) causes you to stiffen against the horse's movement. As a result you might find that it is more difficult to feel the hind feet. Or you might notice that you tend to rock sideways or collapse on one side of your rib cage. The bottom line is that once the leg is braced against the stirrup (instead of receiving the motion of the horse through a soft knee joint) the rider is no longer within the motion of the horse.

A supple knee that sinks down is important when following the motion of the walk and it is critical toward achieving an independent lower leg and to be able to sit the trot, rise to the trot correctly, and sit the canter. Finding the motion of your knee sinking back/down during the walk while having your feet in the stirrups means that your joints can function within the fixed distance of the stirrup leather or fender. Therefore, the joints of your hip, knee, ankle, and toes adjust to remain within this "frame." Pushing your feet out alters the frame of both you and your horse. It will often cause the horse to hollow his back because the weight of your seat is no longer supported through your legs, it is concentrated instead in your feet and therefore in your stirrups. In most cases this will cause the horse to tense his back and impair the quality of his movement. Practicing to soften the back of the knee is important toward future work.

PUT ALL FOUR FEET TOGETHER

Once you have found the feeling of the front feet it is time to put all four feet together. Generally, the first time someone attempts to count out all four feet they remain stuck in the "1, 2, 1, 2" count of just the front or hind feet. In fact, in the time it takes to count

Figure 3

gaited horse that is supposed to pace.) So it is important to remain aware of the quality of your horse's walk and that it always has four distinct beats.

Now that you can feel all four feet you will be able to monitor the quality of the walk. As the horse increases the degree of collection the walk must remain four-beat. If you stiffen your hips and restrict your joints it will be more difficult for the horse to remain fluid. By continuing to feel the four feet, as you have been able to do in the above exercise, you can keep the walk quality and increase collection through your seat and back. The depth of swing from the hind feet under the body must continue as the horse raises his withers and back to collect. This means that the rib cage must lift in order to provide the space for the hind legs (more on how to do this later).

The rider can feel the movement of the horse's rib cage through the lower leg. Developing a soft hinge for a knee joint allows the lower leg of the rider to swing freely and therefore follow the horse's barrel. If the knees are stiff then the barrel will swing away from the lower leg and you will lose the contact and feel for the horse's sides.

Notice that as the horse walks on a long rein the horse's barrel swings left and right. The swinging motion tells you what the hind legs are doing. The barrel swings away from the hind leg that is advancing underneath you. Feel how there is an alternate swing left, right, left, right in your lower leg. If you let your seat become involved with this swing then you will have too much lateral movement. Instead, remember to keep the forward-back movement in your seat and only let the lower leg follow the barrel left and right. Your knee and thigh will continue to sink back and down as the lower leg follows the barrel back and under.

out just the front or hind feet, the other two feet have moved. The count for all four feet then is double time. "1, 2, 3, 4, 1, 2, 3, 4." Again, it is a good idea to go to a hard surface and listen to the footfalls. Then see if you can match up the feeling of all four feet to the sound. Don't worry at first about which foot you are counting. Just get into the rhythm of it. Later you can do the exercise by beginning on a specific foot and counting each foot. Remember that the walk has both lateral and diagonal elements to it so when you count the specific feet it will be left hind, left front, right hind, right front, left hind, left front, etc. Depending on the quality of the walk this could feel more or less lateral.

A walk that has been "broken" becomes a pace (both legs on the same side moving together) (Fig. 3). The horse loses the four-beat nature of the stride and it becomes laterally two-beat. This pacing walk can be caused by a number of things: poor saddle fit impeding the withers, holding the horse's head and driving with the seat into the hands, and/or faulty shoeing to name a few. It can be a difficult fault to correct. (Note, however, that this is different than a

See what happens if you increase the intensity of the back/under swing of the lower leg by putting a slight emphasis on the movement. Think of it more like sending a ping-pong ball across the net rather than trying to shove the barrel across. You want to give an impulse that moves the barrel rather than physically trying to move it. Notice that by increasing the impulse of your lower leg in rhythm to the horse, the walk increases and the horse strides out more. If you decrease the impulse and reduce the forward back motion in your seat you can decrease the walk.

If you walk on a circle notice if the barrel swings more toward the middle of the circle or more toward the outside of the circle. If the horse is bending correctly there will be slightly more swing to the outside. If he is leaning in through his rib cage, thereby not following the line of the circle, then his rib cage will swing more toward the middle of the circle. By slightly increasing the emphasis of the rib cage swing you can increase the degree of bend in the horse.

The lower leg follows the movement of the horse's ribcage.

21

The Aids at the Trot

SO FAR, WE HAVE DEFINED GOOD TIMING AS USING YOUR AIDS AT the appropriate moment within the movement of the horse to achieve the desired result with a minimum of effort. To time your aids correctly you need to know what part of the horse's body is moving throughout the walk cycle. With that in mind, we've looked at the walk in terms of "what is happening when." Then we talked about what the rider might feel during the different phases of the walk.

Hopefully you have gone out in between readings and experimented with these concepts. If you have, by now you can feel all four feet at a walk. You know what phase of the stride each foot is in when you have a particular feeling in your seat and you can influence the quality of your horse's walk by using your body to enhance or inhibit the pattern.

You may have come up with your own images and feelings to describe the movement of your horse's walk. Descriptions of feelings are as unique as each individual and horse. Two ways that my students have described the feelings experienced during the walk are: walking on top of a walking horse, and "feeling like you are so 'into' the horse that your legs and his legs are working together."

It would be useful to come up with your own unique word or phrase that helps you capture the overall movement of walk within your body. This way you transfer the exercises from the left-brained activity of looking at all the little details to the right-brained conceptual side of your mind. By creating a single word, image, or feeling you can access all the detail in an instant. This will make the feeling much more accessible if you lose it or when you ride a different horse, rather than trying to recall all the individual steps.

Think of all the exercises we have done so far as creating a language. The details we have covered are the letters of the alphabet: front leg, hind leg, support, flight, landing, and breakover phase of the stride. Once you have a bunch of letters you can spell words like walk, slow, halt, etc. You won't have to rebuild the letter each time you need it to create another word because you have already studied the letter enough to understand it. As we continue with this series, adding new words to your vocabulary, we will refer back to the letters we have already defined. Some of the new words might get quite complicated. As long as you have already learned the necessary letters, the

larger words, sentences, phrases, and paragraphs become quite easy.

Sometimes you might discover that you missed a letter back in the beginning. Therefore, when you tried to spell a word it did not produce the desired result (you or your horse got confused). That's OK because you can always go back, learn that missing letter, then spell the new word or sentence clearly and correctly. With the concept of understanding letters to build words you will begin to see that the "problem" is simply a lack of "letters" rather than "resistance" on the part of the horse. He is trying to understand your language based on the letters you have explained to him. Or you might be trying to do an exercise and suddenly realize you missed the necessary letters, words, or sentences to teach your horse a certain phrase.

In the creation of your right-brained conceptual map, if a single word or image is too abbreviated for you to produce your desired body pattern within yourself or your horse then a series of words, sounds, or feelings might be necessary. Riders often develop a "checklist" of four or five key points that they play over in their mind to re-create the total feeling they are looking for. I suggest that you keep these words, images, or feelings short and lyrical, like a rhyme, to make them easily accessible. Then simply "sing" this rhyme over and over until it becomes an unconscious positive habit. Repeat this exercise with each new task you attempt.

Let's continue now and look at the trot. You might recall that the trot is a two-beat gait. The other two-beat gait is a pace (see Fig. 3, page 104). The difference between trot and pace is that in trot the horse moves diagonal pairs of legs (left front, right hind; right front, left hind) together. In the pace the pair of legs on the same side (left front, left hind; right front, right hind) move together. Unlike the walk, there is a moment of suspension in the trot. Suspension is when all four feet are off the ground at the same time. A "really bouncy" trot will have a lot of suspension whereas a Western pleasure jog will have very little (if any) suspension.

When we begin to do various exercises at the trot, please remember all the directions given for the walk. Use a quiet horse. Put yourself in a safe environment where you can explore what is happening without having to worry about your surroundings. Have a ground person to help you. If you choose to close your eyes, open them if you feel uncomfortable.

Watch a horse trot on a hard surface and observe the movement of trot. Notice the diagonal pairs of legs moving simultaneously. Observe the moment of suspension between the pairs of legs. Close your eyes and listen to the sound. Remember that the sound will indicate the landing phase of the trot stride. Notice that you only hear two beats "1, 2, 1, 2" as the diagonal pairs of legs land. Listen to how much "space" there is between the sounds of the landing phases. If it is long then there is either a lot of suspension or the horse has a long

stride. If the space is nonexistent there may not be any suspension at all. Also notice if the time between the diagonal pairs of legs is even or uneven. Uneven sounds tell you that a diagonal pair of legs is restricted and may even indicate lameness. Repeat this exercise while mounted. Recall what you saw while watching the horse trot with the feelings you experience while mounted.

When the horse trots, you can either sit the trot, absorbing the diagonal motion and suspension in your seat and legs, or rise to the trot (i.e., "posting"). When the horse's trot has little or no suspension there is very little cause for you to post because the horse does not throw you out of the saddle. A dressage horse, by contrast, typically has a tremendous amount of upward thrust so the riders has to be very strong in her postural muscles to absorb the motion in order to sit the trot. However, when the horse is working properly through the back (rib cage lifting upward filling the rider's seat) it is much easier to sit the trot regardless of the amount of suspension than when the horse trots with the back down.

When posting, the rider rises up and down going in and out of the saddle in

Rising on the "correct" diagonal—as the outside front leg advances.

Rising on the "incorrect" diagonal—as the inside front leg advances.

Landing phase of the right front/left hind and breakover phase of the right hind/left front.

Support phase of the right front/left hind, flight phase of the left front, right hind.

rhythm to the trot. The rider can rise with either diagonal pair of legs. A rider is referred to as "rising on the correct or incorrect diagonal" depending on which diagonal pair of legs is moving when the rider is rising. The terms "correct" or "incorrect" are arbitrary and have been determined by convention. In order to ensure that people did not always rise on the same diagonal pair of legs for extended periods of time it was decided that the "correct" rising diagonal was when the "outside" foreleg ("outside" being the leg near the rail) was moving forward (see photo on page 108, left). When changing direction the rider "changes diagonals." The rider can do this by sitting two beats of the trot or standing for two beats (less weight on the horse's back and a good exercise to test the rider's balance). Now the rider is rising as the other foreleg moves forward. Therefore, the reference to diagonal here is the diagonal pair of legs (not to be confused with changing direction from corner to corner across the diagonal line of the arena). When training the horse, a rider can choose to rise on the "incorrect" diagonal in order to influence the other diagonal pair of legs (see photo on page 108, right). When riding long distances in open country (for instance in endurance rides) it is important to change the posting diagonal regularly in order to evenly distribute the work on both diagonal pairs of legs.

In trot you still have the four different phases of limb movement. The landing phase of the stride is when you hear the hooves hit the ground (right front/left hind) (see photo, top left). The support phase is when you are either sitting or rising if you are doing posting trot as the limbs support the weight and propel the body forward (right front/left hind) (see photo, top right). Breakover is the moment when the diagonal pair of legs is leaving the ground and flight is when the legs are traveling through the air (right front/left hind).

The horse's rib cage can either be down (head high, hollow-backed horse or "swan-necked" horse) or up, allowing the horse to lengthen the neck and put the head down during the trot stride. If the horse's back is down (see top left photo on page 110) the rider will feel like she is constantly being pulled back into a hole. It will be difficult to get out of the saddle to rise to the trot because the horse's back is not supporting the rider. When the back is up (see top right

The horse's back is down so his head has to come up.

The horse's back is coming up, therefore the head is going down.

photo on page 110) the rider is easily supported and can comfortably sit or post the trot with little effort. Therefore it is important to work on getting the horse to lift the back in the trot. We'll get to more on how to do this later.

The rib cage can also be shifted down and sideways. On a circle at the trot (see photo, bottom left) this can cause the horse to fall in or out of the circle line. This problem would most likely have already appeared during the walk. However, on a circle at the trot this seemingly small shift

of the rib cage to the inside becomes much more obvious because now the horse has momentum. When the horse lifts the rib cage up and out so that the withers remain perpendicular to the ground, the horse will track straight and move evenly on a circle. This is referred to as "bending the horse" on a circle. The bend begins in the rib cage just about underneath where the rider is sitting. The horse's neck will reflect this bend by following the curve of the circle. You will see many horses that are supposedly bent by pulling their head

The horse is leaning into the circle with the rib cage and shoulder.

The horse is tracking straight and even on a circle. This will lead to bending, lifting the back, and lowering the head.

around. Pulling the head around will flex the neck but not necessarily shift the rib cage. In this case you have "false bend" and the horse will continue to fall in and/or swing the hindquarters out on the circle instead of tracking straight around the arc of the circle.

Next we will look at how the rider can influence the quality of the trot by accentuating different phases of the stride using a minimum of effort. First, why not go ahead and do a little experimenting yourself and find out what happens. Good luck!

22

The Aids at the Rising Trot

A RIDER CAN EITHER SIT THE TROT, ABSORBING THE MOTION, or post the trot (also called rising the trot). When rising the trot the rider is out of the saddle as one diagonal pair of legs is moving forward and sitting in the saddle as the other pair moves forward. In order to distribute the work evenly between the two diagonal pairs of legs, the rider can change the "rising diagonal" by sitting two beats and then rise again as the other foreleg moves forward. In order to understand how the rider

can influence the trot it is important to know what is happening when.

The sound of the hooves hitting the ground is the landing phase of each diagonal pair of legs. If the rider is rising the trot on the traditionally "correct" diagonal (when the outside foreleg moves forward) then the rider will be up during the flight phase of the inside hind/outside foreleg diagonal pair. ("Inside" and "outside" refer to the legs in relation to a circle or the rail.) When the rider is down in the saddle during rising trot the outside hind and inside foreleg are in flight phase.

Following is a chart of what phase the horse's legs are in during the different phases

Phase of rising trot	Phase of the stride for the diagonal pair of legs

	Rising out of the saddle
	
	Inside hind/outside foreleg—
	    breakover/flight
	Outside hind/inside foreleg—
	    flight/landing

	Top of the rise out of the saddle Inside hind/outside foreleg—flight Outside hind/inside foreleg—support

	Lowering towards the saddle
	
	Inside hind/outside foreleg—
	    flight/landing
	Outside hind/inside foreleg—
	    breakover/flight

	Sitting in the saddle Inside hind/outside foreleg—support Outside hind/inside foreleg—flight

of the rising trot. The description below applies to when the rider is rising as the outside foreleg is moving forward (the "correct" rising diagonal).

Notice that when the rider is rising and lowering the horse's limbs are in the same phase, only it is the opposite pair of legs moving (breakover/flight, flight/landing). This is true also for the top of the rise and the sit phase (flight/support) (Refer back to the photos in Chapter 21.)

Many people have difficulty knowing when they are rising on the "correct" diagonal. The traditional way to determine if you are correct is to look down at the outside shoulder of the horse as you are rising out of the saddle. When you are on the "correct" diagonal you will see the outside foreleg moving forward as you are going up. However, this method doesn't seem to work for some people and it means that you have to look down when you start your rising trot. Looking down causes the rider's weight to fall forward and can throw both the horse and the rider off balance. Therefore, learning to rise on the correct diagonal by feel would be preferable to looking down.

Before attempting to do the following exercise it would be helpful to review the walk lessons in Chapters 19 and 20 feeling

all four feet moving through the different phases of the stride. After you have reviewed those lessons ask your horse to go into a slow trot. (Again, use your quiet horse so you can have some time to explore without having to worry about what the horse is going to do.) You will want a slow enough trot that you can sit comfortably. If you have difficulty sitting the trot, go first to the trot transition exercises later in this chapter and in Chapter 24. Then come back to sitting. After you have been able to do transitions in trot and sit the trot you can again work on rising to the correct diagonal by feeling the hind feet.

At trot, close your eyes briefly and feel the two hind legs pushing up into your seat. Notice the alternating push from each hind leg. If you cannot feel the alternate push up into your seat and your horse is relaxed, place one hand on the point of the inside hip (refer to the illustration on page 97). Feel the horse pushing that hip into your hand. Then place your hand on your own buttocks (same side) between yourself and the saddle and find the feeling of the push into your seat. Rise as you feel the inside hind leg push into your seat. If you follow this push it sends you out of the saddle. Look at the outside shoulder and confirm whether or not you are going up as the outside foreleg is moving forward. Change direction, change hands, and repeat the exercise going the other way.

On a straight line repeatedly change your rising diagonal. If possible, have someone assist you. You can call out which diagonal you think you are on and your assistant can give you feedback as to whether or not you are correct. Test yourself to see if you can do this every four strides, every three strides, and then every two strides. Change the rising diagonal by sitting two beats (the traditional way to change the diagonal). Then see if you can change the rising diagonal by staying out of the saddle for two beats.

The approximate length of a neck strap for assisting the rider at rising trot.

You might want to put a neck strap (you can use a piece of rope or an old stirrup leather) around your horse's neck. That way if you start to lose your balance you can grab for the horn or the neck strap instead of your reins.

Changing your rising diagonal while remaining out of the saddle will test your balance more than sitting the change. This is also a great exercise to improve your balance at the rising trot. Repeat this exercise without using your reins for balance by holding your hands at shoulder height. Make sure you have given your horse enough slack so that you are not pulling on his mouth. Another variation of this exercise is to stay up out of the saddle for two, three, or four beats then continue rising the trot.

If you are in an enclosed environment on a quiet, safe horse and comfortable with having your eyes closed, repeat the exercise of changing your rising diagonal on a straight line closing your eyes every other time. This will help you to feel the diagonal pair of legs. Notice the difference in the thrust of the two hind feet as you rise on one diagonal and then the other. Do they feel similar? Often you will notice that the horse has a "strong" hind leg and a "weak" hind leg. He will push off harder with the strong leg. Typically this stronger hind leg is the left hind.

Next ride a large circle continuing to change your rising diagonal at regular intervals (four, three, or two strides). Feel how different the two diagonals are when you ride the circle. Change direction and repeat the two exercises (straight lines, large circles). Has the feeling in the diagonal pairs of legs changed with direction? Often the horse will feel more balanced in one direction than the other. If you are not sure which direction feels more balanced, find out by changing directions several times. Which way does he fall in or out? Is that the same direction as the weaker feeling you noticed

on the straight line? Give yourself plenty of time to simply feel the difference in the horse's movement without worrying about which diagonal you are on. Then notice which feels better and if you are on the "correct" rising diagonal. What happens when you change diagonals?

As you go through these different exercises you might notice that the two diagonals begin to feel more and more alike. You may also notice that your horse is getting straighter and leaning less through the turns. Oftentimes we get into a rut doing the same thing over and over. The horses also get into habits, which they repeat as well. Sometimes the horse is the one who keeps putting us on the same diagonal because he is uncomfortable pushing with the other hind leg. By changing things a bit you make yourself and your horse more aware of your old habits. Asking the horse to adapt to the shifts in position and balance by changing rising diagonals can result in a more even, steady trot.

Another good way to develop a rhythmic trot is to use a small clip-on type metronome. You can clip it to your clothes or the saddle. A good rising trot is between 138–144 beats per minute. The steady tempo of the metronome gives the rider something to listen to for the rising trot. Horses will also adjust to the sound. In fact it is not unusual to see horses perform much better when there is music playing in the arena. The music provides a steady rhythm and beat for everyone.

In addition, there is a way to time your aids so that you rise on the correct diagonal with the first stride of trot from walk every time. If your horse is sensitive to your trot aids this will be easy. Going from walk to trot will be like adding the last drop of water into a glass, which causes it to overflow. If you have to kick and shove several times before the horse trots, this exercise probably will not work at first. In the former case the trot is ready to happen and it will only take a breath

A good walk is necessary for an easy transition to the trot. Ask as the inside front leg is landing; lengthen through your spine and think "trot."

The inside hind leg has already pushed off causing the rider to ride on the correct diagonal on the first beat of the trot.

to create it. You will be totally prepared for the first trot stride. In the latter case, you are too busy trying to make your horse move so you won't be balanced and ready for anything. You will need to create a marching walk first before you can do this exercise.

From the walk ask the horse to trot as the inside foreleg is landing (your inside knee and thigh will be just beginning to sink back and down). The inside hind leg, which is entering the support phase, is next to push off the ground. The push from the inside hind leg begins the trot. The outside foreleg is already in flight so it continues to advance forward. Begin to rise with the push from the inside hind leg and you will be on the correct diagonal every time! Remember that you have to have a good marching walk for this to work correctly (see top photo). There is only a split second between the landing phase of the inside front leg and the push from the inside hind leg.

You might want to come back to this exercise after you have been through the section on lengthening (Part Four). When you are ready for the trot (i.e., you have a good marching walk) think lengthening up through the top of your head. This will be enough to create the trot transition.

If your horse is unwilling to push off the inside hind leg you might feel a delay in the response to your trot aids. It may feel like you are getting pulled back into the saddle as you try to rise. The horse hesitates as he adjusts himself, then pushes off with the outside hind leg. If you rise at that moment you will wind up on the "incorrect" diagonal. If your horse hesitates you could wait an extra beat before you rise to get back in sync with the correct diagonal but the problem is the horse was not prepared to push off with the inside hind leg when you asked. You must create the trot long before you ask for it. Prepare by creating a marching walk with impulsion so when you say "now" with your aids the horse will be ready to push off into trot. Remember the different phases of the stride are as follows:

Support — the leg is on the ground. As the horse's body advances over it, the leg pushes off the ground.

Breakover — the moment when the foot leaves the ground.

Flight — the leg is traveling through the air.

Landing — the moment when the foot strikes the ground.

23

How the Aids Influence the Quality of the Trot

*I*N CHAPTER 22, WE REVIEWED THE HORSE'S LEG SEQUENCE IN TROT. Then we looked at how the rider finds the correct trot rising diagonal. In summary the rider needs to have a sufficiently forward walk so that there is very little effort needed to change the stride to trot.

Then, by asking for trot when the inside foreleg is landing, the rider can strike off in trot on the correct rising diagonal. For this exercise to work it is very important that the walk is active and marching.

Remember that a good walk is comprised of the horse stepping

This horse's back is down creating a hole for the rider and throwing her into a "chair seat." This makes it very difficult for the rider to rise to the trot without great effort.

deeply underneath the rib cage with the hind legs and lifting up through the back. This will help to raise the withers and lengthen the neck out and down. If the horse is not working through his back there will be a lot of sideways swing through the horse's midsection. Whether standing or moving the back sinks and there is little to no forward impulsion coming through the topline. The horse will not push from behind upward into the trot. Instead he will shuffle or fall forward into the trot. The rider often sits the first beat or two and may have a difficult time getting onto the correct diagonal at the initiation of the trot. Sitting this trot, the rider will feel a lot of side-to-side drop in their pelvis rather than a straight and forward, upward lifting feeling through the seat. The side-to-side motion is created by the horse swinging the rib cage down and sideways to bring the hind legs under rather than raising the rib cage up.

Although riding a horse with a dropped back at a slow trot may seem comfortable to you, it is really hard on the horse. Remember the example a while back of having your

friend go on all fours and placing your hands on her back while it was down or up? You could apply a tremendous amount of pressure on the back when it was up but very little when it was down. Well this is the same thing in the horse only now at the trot. When the back is down the horse's midsection is strung like a hammock between the four posts (the legs). The weight of the rider causes the back to sag further especially if the rider is sitting with her legs pushed out in front of her (see photo). This stress would be similar to you hiking with a poorly fitted backpack full of rocks on your back. The dead weight pulls you down, makes your back sore, and fatigues your hips and legs.

The rock-filled backpack scenario is the same for the horse. Instead of the horse efficiently supporting the load, the skeletal, ligament, and tendon system is working inefficiently. The horse will labor in the trot, fall on the forehand, be extremely uncomfortable to sit at a faster trot, tire far more easily, and is more likely to have lameness problems due to poor use of his back. In fact, a horse that moves with his back down may often have "mysterious traveling lameness." This is a lameness that seems to keep shifting from leg to leg because the actual cause of the problem is a sore back.

When a horse is using his back correctly (lifting the back to bring the hind legs under) the horse can support weight on the long back muscles and bounce off the ground in a way that is similar to dribbling a basketball. Whether you are traveling down court (lengthening the stride) or slowly walking toward the basket springing the ball upward into your hand (collected trot), the ball spends more time in the air then it does touching the floor because it is rebounding off the ground. Depending on how the horse moves his legs, he may still have a very flat feeling through the back in sitting trot (little undulation of the midsection common in

Thoroughbreds and Quarter Horses) and still be working up through the back. Or the horse may have a really "bouncy" trot (Warmbloods) with greater undulation of the midsection. Nonetheless, when the horse's back is up it is much easier to sit the trot regardless of the type of trot the horse has. Also, the weight of the rider will be borne through lengthening the back which decreases the work placed on the limbs.

If the trot has a lot of suspension (time when all four legs are off the ground) the time of the flight phase increases. The rider will feel the horse send him out of the saddle (if rising the trot) for a longer period of time. If the flight phase is longer because the stride length has increased, the horse will cover a longer distance, more like dribbling down court. As the horse increases the stride the rider will have to adjust to avoid being thrown backward by the increase thrust of the hind limb. This feeling is similar to sitting on the back of a motorcycle and having the driver accelerate rapidly. You have to be ready to absorb the transitional force of acceleration by lengthening forward and up as the horse pushes (see Part Four on lengthening).

If there is very little suspension then the support phase will be much longer. Think of a Western pleasure horse's jog, which has almost no suspension. There is a very long support phase for each diagonal pair of legs. This is one of the reasons why the trot is so smooth and difficult to post. It is designed to be soft and smooth so that there is very little jarring of the rider whereas the dressage horse is designed to have a large, powerful, floating trot stride with lots of suspension. Most riders have to learn to sit this trot in order not to interfere with the horse. To use the analogy of the ball, the Western pleasure horse is like trying to dribble a half-inflated basketball. It just doesn't want to come off the ground so

This horse's back is up and supporting the rider in the trot.

there is little to no rebound. The flight phase is drastically reduced, the stride may be shortened, and the support phase is greatly increased. The dressage horse in passage (collected trot with increased cadence and suspension) has a long flight phase, a decreased length of stride because the stride is so elevated, and a very short support phase. A horse with a shorter stride will have less time between footfalls. A horse with a quick, choppy trot can be compared to a sewing machine and the rider will feel like she is rapidly going up/down in the rising trot.

Now let's relate this to what we can observe while riding. The sound of the trot (landing phase) will change depending upon the length of the stride in the trot. If the horse has a long time between footfalls the horse has either a longer stride or a more suspended stride. If the footfalls sound close together then there is very little flight phase in the trot. Notice the sound of your horse's trot. Is it a long time between footfalls, a short time, or something in between? Is there an even rhythm? If it is not even and rhythmic, then one diagonal pair of legs may be taking a shorter step than the other pair. When rising to the trot notice if there is an uneven sound to the trot; your rising may also be uneven. In other words, the uneven sound is telling you that a diagonal pair of legs is not moving the same distance as the other pair of legs. This will cause you to return to the saddle quicker on one rising diagonal.

If you feel like you fall back into the saddle on one diagonal more than the other, it may be the result of that diagonal pair hitting the ground faster than the other pair. One hind leg is probably coming to the ground sooner, therefore not stepping as deeply underneath the horse's barrel (and your body). The result is that your weight is not being supported by the horse's push through the leg and back. Instead of the horse lifting the back into your seat, he is dropping his back. If you are not in balance (i.e., your feet are pushed out in front of you) you will fall back into the hole created by the dropped back of the horse. It will become difficult to get out of the saddle for the next stride so your timing will be off.

Falling back into the hole can become a serious issue toward timing the aids correctly. Think of it like this. If you went to sit on your favorite really comfortable, soft chair (horse with poor muscle tone in the back, weak abdominals, and dropped ribcage) and put your feet a little out in front of you, how easy would it be to get out of the chair? But if you were sitting on a hard level bench with a cushion on it (horse with a firm back) how quickly could you get up off the bench?

Getting trapped into the hole of a weak-backed horse is like the soft chair. The horse with a good back that is well muscled and who carries the back up is like the bench. The weak-backed horse generally is not pushing forward from behind and is not reaching deep underneath the body. This is part of the problem.

A rider that is out of balance (feet pushed out in front, bracing on the stirrups) can cause the horse to drop the back. This person will spend more time in the sitting phase of rising trot than the rising phase. In addition the leg pushed out in front creates a lever that the rider has to get up and over to get off the horse's back (again, try to get out of the soft chair with feet out in front).

If the rider were to bring her legs underneath her body and focus on rising more evenly up and down to the trot, the horse would be able to step deeper underneath him and have a longer, more balanced stride. In many cases this will be sufficient to allow the horse to lift the back and the rider up. If the horse is moving unevenly in the diagonal pair of legs, the rider will fall back into the hole on one side but not the other. This can throw the rider into a twist. To correct this problem the rider has to take care not to go down into the hole. Instead the rider needs to carry herself as if there were no hole so the horse will have the opportunity to rise up through the back and fill the hole. But if the rider keeps falling into the hole it drives the back down and the hind leg out behind the horse.

24

Walk-Trot-Walk Transitions

W E'VE LOOKED AT HOW THE HORSE CAN USE HIS BACK WHEN

trotting. By now you may be asking yourself why all

this discussion about the horse's back being up or

down, diagonal pairs of legs even

or uneven, and rider position in

neutral with the feet underneath

vs. out in front? The answer to

this question depends on the

quality of the transitions you are

looking for. If you want smooth,

even, flowing, and responsive

transitions you need to be in

The horse has a good walk preceding the transition to trot. Notice that the inside hind leg is stepping deeply underneath the horse's body. The rider has her legs underneath her body as she asks the horse to trot.

The rider is ahead of the motion in the transition from walk to trot. She has rounded her back, drawn her legs up, and pitched forward with the upper body during the transition. Also, she has tightened her arms and is almost pulling herself up with the reins to get out of the saddle for rising trot. Notice that she will not be on the correct diagonal unless she sits two beats before rising.

has everything to do with the quality of that transition. If the horse is in balance, light, and forward then the transitions become simple, effortless, and require a minimum of aids. Remember the analogy of adding the last drop of water to the glass that causes it to overflow.

If the horse is on the forehand, heavy, unbalanced, and not forward, the transitions will become kicking and pulling matches. The rider needs to be in balance so that the horse does not have to compensate for the rider before performing the transition.

When you are out of alignment with gravity your timing will be late. You become a weight the horse has to "catch" before he can perform the desired move. Similarly, the horse has to be in alignment, his back up, and straight through the spine, so that he can respond immediately to your requests.

This horse/rider balance is very much like dancing with a good vs. a bad dance partner. A good male dance partner, the rider, is always supportive and leading the woman into the next movement by simply guiding her. A bad male partner is rough, uncoordinated, stepping on the woman's toes, and throwing her all over the place.

A good woman dance partner (the horse) responds to the subtle inferences of the man (rider). She is balanced and poised so that it takes little effort to spin her around, go forward or back, and move her feet at speed. Similarly dancing with a poor female dancer (horse out of balance) is like trying to drag a sack of grain across the floor.

In order to be a good dance partner you need to remain in alignment with your feet underneath you during the transition to trot. That way you will not hinder the horse at the moment of the transition. You will be able to aid the horse into trot making the transition look light and easy. Your timing

alignment with gravity so that you do not become a burden to your horse.

So now we are going to look at how to ride balanced walk-trot-walk transitions. The quality of the gait preceding the transition will be accurate within the stride rather than too early or delayed.

To ride a smooth transition from walk to trot you want your horse to be responsive to both your leg and seat aids. With your pelvis in a neutral position the trot aids can be as subtle as gently squeezing the lower part of your buttocks while lengthening up through your back to the top of your head (lengthening is covered in detail in Part Four). This action brings your pelvis slightly more underneath you.

At the same time let your legs lengthen down activating the hamstring (the muscles at the back of the thigh) and calf muscles. This closes your legs on the horse. The feeling is similar to giving your horse a hug with the inside of your legs. This movement opens the hip joints at the front of the socket, advancing your seat bones forward underneath you. This feeling may be similar to Power Position (Chapter 15) when someone pulls on your reins.

Time your trot aids as the inside foreleg is landing on the ground. If you are going to sit the trot it is less important which foreleg you are observing. However if you want to rise on the correct diagonal from the very first stride of trot it will make a difference (see previous chapter).

Remember the walk sequence—inside hind, inside fore, outside hind, outside foreleg. The inside hind leg is in position to push off the ground as the inside foreleg lands on the ground. Aiding for the trot and rising at that moment means that the inside hind will push off and unify with the outside foreleg into the first diagonal pair of legs. You will be on the correct diagonal from the very first trot stride. Again remember your horse needs to be light and responsive to your trot aids for this to work because you will be going up for the first rising stride as he pushes off the outside hind leg.

Here the rider is with the motion of the horse at walk. As the inside foreleg lands she is lengthening up through her spine to the top of her head in order to remain in balance for the transition. By asking for trot as the inside foreleg lands the inside hind leg will push for the first stride of trot.

The rider rose as the horse pushed off with the inside hind leg. This automatically begins the rising trot on the correct diagonal (outside foreleg moving forward). Notice in this photo that the rider has remained upright throughout the transition. She is allowing the horse to push her up out of the saddle by receiving the forward push from the horse created in the walk. She allows her hip joints to open and her leg to remain underneath her body by lengthening up through the top of her head as the horse moves forward into trot.

Look again at the photos on this page. Notice that in the top photo the inside foreleg has already landed. The rider is cueing the horse to trot. In the bottom photo the

The rider is behind the motion in the transition to trot. Her upper body has fallen behind the vertical so she will be thrown back as the horse move forward into trot. Then she will have to "catch up" to the motion in order to reestablish balance.

The rider has sat back into the saddle, braced the feet out in front, and pulled on the reins to bring the horse from trot to walk. Notice that the horse braced with the outside foreleg and the outside hind leg is trailing. This prevents the outside hind leg from supporting the horse's body weight. Therefore the first stride of walk will be heavy and on the forehand.

inside hind leg has now pushed off the ground and the diagonal pair of legs (inside hind/outside fore) are traveling through the air. The rider has risen as that inside hind leg pushed off.

By applying a firm pressure with your lower legs underneath you, you stabilize your body to rise at that moment when you feel the push from the inside hind leg. This is going to require some practice. If the horse refuses to go forward you will need to help out with a slightly stronger leg aid—a tap of your stick or the tail of your mecate—so that he understands that this is your signal to go forward into trot.

It is really important that you don't alter your position when you use these other aids. If you drastically increase your seat by pushing and shoving to get the horse to trot you put yourself in an unstable position. In addition, you teach the horse not to respond to the light aid you asked with first. Shoving with the seat may cause the horse to drop the back so that it is even more difficult to get the transition, never mind timing your rising to the inside foreleg.

By kicking with your legs you might find that you are not ready when the horse does trot. If the horse trots when you have pulled your legs away to kick you will be unstable and likely to pitch forward or fall behind as the horse moves out. This punishes the horse in the back and mouth for performing the transition to trot. Instead of making your horse more responsive, he becomes dull.

The key to the upward transition is to ask as that inside foreleg is landing. Keep your body in position. Look ahead so that you maintain balance. Lengthen up through your spine. If you need to add more pressure for the trot, maintain your body position by adding additional aids.

If you miss the transition on that stride wait till the next stride and ask again. This won't be but a moment later (remember the walk sequence) so you have to remain ready, keep the walk balanced, and catch the next stride right away. Remember you can increase the strength of your aids without altering your body position if you need more help to get the trot. You might consider whether you had a good strong, forward walk first in preparation for the trot before you put all the blame on the horse's lack of willingness to trot.

Another caution is not to repeat this too often. You don't want to take the horse beyond the point of responsiveness into dullness. You want to keep the movements fresh and alive. So do a few repetitions then move onto trot circles, then come back to the transitions again.

For the down transition from trot to walk you will reverse your aid sequence. The horse needs to coil into the joints of the hind leg rather than push. As you ride the down transition from rising trot to walk you will need to absorb the motion in your own joints. This means you have to soften your legs and buttocks slightly letting them melt down into the horse rather than tensing them as we did in the upward transition to trot. If you let go of all the tone in your buttocks, you will crash into the horse's back like a stone and cause him to hollow his back!

It is helpful to ride the transition slowly to get the feel of absorbing the motion with your joints. In the rising trot start to make your rising slower and lower yet continue to rise to the trot. Then make your rising larger and quicker again so that the horse moves out. Do this several times until you can feel the horse coming with you by increasing or decreasing his trot. Remember that slower and lower is not slumping. Keep your body aligned and keep your head and neck aligned over your feet.

Continue to make your rising trot slower and lower until the horse comes back to walk. By doing this exercise you keep yourself in balance during the downward transition and learn how you can do transitions within the trot. If you stiffen any of the joints

Preparation for the transition from trot to walk. The rider is asking the horse to walk as the outside hind leg lands. This places the outside hind leg in support so that it can coil and absorb the momentum of the horse.

The horse is able to maintain his balance through the transition so that he can step deeply underneath with the inside hind on the very first stride of walk.

in your legs you will find that you can't keep your balance. You might even fall back into the saddle, brace against your stirrups, or pull on the horse's mouth.

Change your rising diagonal on the rising phase of trot by staying up for two beats.

When you get this exercise right you will sit only at the moment when the horse takes the first step of walk without the use of the reins. Once you can perform this exercise you will be ready to sit the transitions from the trot to walk. Instead of bracing in your hips to stop the horse you will absorb the motion of the trot so that the horse returns to walk with a minimum of effort and no loss of balance. In this way you will be ready on the next stride to trot on again if you choose rather than having to regroup for a few strides before you can trot out.

After the transition to walk re-create a forward marching walk then do your trot transition again. It is important to return to the marching walk in order to have enough impulsion for a good trot transition. If your down transition was timed correctly you will have a good walk from the first stride.

Continue doing walk/trot/walk transitions. Gradually decrease the number of walk strides before trotting again. See if you can get it down to only two or three strides. If the horse anticipates the exercise continue in the gait you are in (walk or trot) until he settles. Then ask for another transition. Test

yourself to see that you can do the transitions without tipping forward or back as you change the gait. If you are truly in balance you will remain vertical during all the transitions. Also see if you can feel the inside shoulder coming back when you ask for trot so you begin rising on the correct diagonal. Feel for the landing of the outside hind in the down transitions.

Next, test your ability to control your balance in rising trot by doing "touch-and-goes" (almost walk then trot out again). Start at the trot. Begin to return to the walk. On the very last stride of trot, just when the horse would walk, ask the horse to trot on again. Do this by lengthening and increasing your rising.

When you did the touch-and-goes did you go with the horse or did you pitch forward or back as he accelerated? If you can go with the increased trot then you are in balance with your horse and your timing to move out will be pretty accurate. It is important to keep your head and neck lengthening forward and up through transition in line with your body. If you fall back or pitch forward then you are most likely stiffening and interfering with your horse's balance. This will cause your timing to be off and confuse the horse rather than help him.

Notice also that when you can do a good touch-and-go the horse will be relaxed, quiet, forward, and straight. He will push strongly from either hind leg. You can increase or decrease the trot with a minimum of effort. Transitions from trot to walk will be a lot easier now because you are able to absorb the trot motion, which dampens the push of the hind legs. Once you learn to dampen the horse's movement you will be able to ride smooth transitions without using the reins.

Another good exercise to improve your overall balance in the trot is to change your rising diagonal in the air rather than in the sitting phase of rising trot. To do this stay up for two beats then post again. If you find this difficult at first then this will be an excellent exercise for you. It will develop your overall balance. This balance is important when you want to really open up the horse's stride. If you can't change your diagonal by staying up out of the saddle, check to see if you are pushing into your stirrups. This can push your leg forward and cause you to fall back into the saddle making this exercise quite difficult.

Once you find your leg underneath you this exercise will become easy. Practice changing your rising diagonal every six strides. Then reduce it gradually a stride at a time until you can do it to every two strides. Go back to changing the diagonal by sitting and see which way allows your horse to continue without interrupting the trot rhythm. Ultimately you want the horse to remain trotting smoothly when changing diagonal either standing or sitting.

By doing these exercises you will have a better overall balance through walk/trot transitions. The horse will be able to stay in an even rhythm underneath you and you will be able to influence the gait with a minimum of effort. When you are really good, you can get these transitions down to just your breath. Simply breathe in on the up and out on the down as you remain in balance with the horse. I am sure your horse will enjoy the improvement just like we enjoy a good dance partner.

The Aids at the Lope or Canter

U NDERSTANDING THE LOPE OR CANTER STRIDE IS IMPORTANT IN ORDER to correctly time transitions into and out of canter, adjust speed, and execute clear flying changes. (For writing and reading ease, I will refer to both the lope and canter as simply canter.)

When the rider can pick out the repeating patterns of the horse's legs at the canter she will be able to determine which lead the horse is on and time her aids within the canter stride. Timing the aids within the canter (instead of against the movement) will result in more subtle signals and a quieter horse. In order to accomplish this timing, the rider must remain in balance with the horse.

The canter is a three-beat gait. Gallop is different from canter in that it is faster and it is a four-beat gait. In gallop, each leg strikes the ground separately due to the greater stride length and speed. If the canter is four-beat, it is typically considered incorrect.

The three beats of the canter are like a waltz. When you listen to the canter you hear the "one, two, three, one, two, three" rhythm of the gait. This sound is the landing phase of the stride. There will usually be a pause between the third beat and the first beat of the next stride. The pause indicates the moment of suspension, when all four feet are off the ground at the same time.

The degree of suspension in the canter stride depends upon the breed of horse, the

amount of collection in which the horse is ridden, and the quality of the gait. Tennessee Walkers have a very upright, rocking motion to the canter. Upper level dressage horses have a round canter due to the lift in their backs. This roundness indicates a greater degree of collection resulting in a longer period of suspension. Quarter Horses tend to have a flatter canter with less suspension. Remember that suspension is the time the all the legs are off the ground.

Again, listen to a horse cantering. Close your eyes to get a better feel for the rhythm. Pick out the "1, 2, 3" waltz pattern. How much of a gap do you hear between the third beat of one stride and the first beat of the next? This will tell you how much suspension the horse has. Notice that you might also hear the horse breathing in rhythm to the canter stride. The relaxed horse will make a soft snorting sound once per stride. This is because the hind limbs

Right Lead Canter

Beat of Canter	"1"	"2"	"3"	Suspension
LH	landing/support	support/breakover	flight	flight
RH/LF	flight	landing/support	breakover/flight	flight
RF	flight	flight	landing/support	flight

Left Lead Canter

Beat of Canter	"1"	"2"	"3"	Suspension
RH	landing/support	support/break-over	flight	flight
LH/RF	flight	landing/support	break-over/flight	flight
LF	flight	flight	landing/support	flight

LH—left hind leg; RH—right hind leg; LF—left front leg; RF—right front leg drive the horse's diaphragm like a piston creating the sound on expiration.

IDENTIFYING PROBLEMS IN THE CANTER

Listen to different horses canter and see if you can pick out the three beats. In some horses you might notice that instead of the beats being well separated and distinct it sounds like all the feet hit the ground relatively close together followed by a long pause. If this is the case, the horse most likely has a high head carriage and a hollow back rather than a rounded back. I think of this canter as a two-beat canter or a "down, up" canter.

The first beat of a "down, up canter" is when all the feet hit the ground in relatively close succession. The second beat is the suspension phase. Often this type of canter will be very lateral in appearance. In other words, the hind and front legs on

I am riding the first beat of right-lead canter, the landing phase of outside hind leg. I am sitting with my legs underneath my body and my seat bones pointing straight down. There is a slight closing of my hip joint as Blondie brings her hind end underneath her by closing her hip joints.

the same side look similar to a pace in that they are almost moving together. Some high-headed jumpers will have a pace-like canter as well. You might even notice the rider posting the canter.

When a horse has a round appearance over the back and a clear three-beat canter with a moment of suspension, he is using his back correctly. Unlike trot the horse needs to lift the back and withers to canter properly. Lifting through the back and withers allows the horse to bring the hind legs underneath the body.

If there is anything pinching the withers (a poorly fitting saddle being one of the primary causes) the horse will not want to lift up through the back and/or withers. In this case the horse will have a flatter canter stride and less suspension. The horse will want to put his head in the air instead of down. Often the horse being pinched in the back and withers will rush forward with a hollow back in the canter and be difficult to slow down or stop unless you pull hard on the reins. Conversely some horses with sore backs and withers are nearly impossible to get into the canter. They associate the back movement required in canter with pain and therefore won't move forward.

In each case—the horse that rushes off at canter or the reluctant horse or the horse with the two-beat type canter—it is important to check that the saddle allows the horse the ability to raise his back. Otherwise you are forcing the horse to work into the pain. An ill-fitting saddle forces the horse's back down while he is trying to lift it up in canter. The horse will have to compensate in his movement which can lead to lameness issues later on.

When the horse is able to lift properly through the back, the head and neck will naturally come down. The withers act like a suspension girder for the musculature at the base of the neck. By lifting through the withers the base of the neck is lifted, raising the sternum up and allowing the neck to lengthen out and down. Hence the horse will no longer brace forward on the sternum making it unnecessary to tie the horse's head down.

The three-beat nature of canter is created by an asymmetry in the pattern of leg movement. Recall that the trot is a symmetrical gait with diagonal pairs of legs moving evenly. The three beats of the canter result from separating one of the diagonal pairs of legs. Therefore instead of a "one, two" count you have a "one, two, three" count.

This asymmetry means that the horse has two different "leads" depending upon which diagonal pair of legs has separated. It is commonly accepted that the "correct" lead on a circle is when the inside foreleg advances separately from the diagonally opposite hind leg. When tracking to the right the horse is said to be on the "right lead" when the right foreleg lands separately from the left hind. When tracking to the left the horse is on the "left lead" when the left foreleg lands separately from the right hind. (The photos in this chapter show right-lead canter.)

Counter-canter is when the rider intentionally asks the horse to canter on the opposite lead from the direction of travel. When tracking to the right the horse is on the left lead. When tracking left the horse is on the right lead. This is an excellent exercise to develop balance in the canter. It is also useful in preparing the horse for flying lead changes (changing from one lead to the other during canter). In order to influence the canter it is important to understand where each leg is during the canter stride. Remember that the different phases of the stride are:

In this photo Blondie is in the second beat of right-lead canter. The diagonal pair of legs—right hind/left front are in support. The left hind leg is in break-over about to start flight phase. The leading leg—right front is at the end of flight phase. Again, I am sitting vertically in the saddle with my leg underneath me. My hip joints have opened to the neutral position.

The third beat of right-lead canter. Here Blondie's leading leg, the right foreleg, is in support. The diagonal pair of legs is in flight and the left hind leg is at the end of flight phase. Notice that Blondie's body has lowered in front during the support phase of the lead leg. I allow Blondie to undulate during this phase of the canter stride by letting my hip joints open past neutral keeping my body in a vertical position. If I did not let my hip joints open then I would tip forward and force Blondie onto the forehand.

Support—the leg is on the ground. As the horse's body advances over it, the leg pushes off the ground.

Breakover—the moment when the foot leaves the ground.

Flight—the leg is traveling through the air.

Landing—the moment when the foot strikes the ground.

A visual way to determine the lead you are on is to glance down while you are cantering. Look to see if the horse's knee of the inside foreleg is "leading." The downside of looking is that it drops your body weight forward and often disturbs the canter. If you must look try to glance with your eyes and not your body.

It is better to be able to "feel" which lead you are on rather than look down. Notice that when you are cantering the horse's head undulates downward as he breaks over the lead leg. This rocking motion of the canter can be useful for you to feel the correct lead.

To feel the three beats of canter start out on a quiet horse in a safe environment where you can focus on what you are doing. Remember that in order to feel the movements of the horse you need to be able to relax and breathe. If you are stiff, tense, and holding your breath then it will be next to impossible to pick out the different legs.

Also remember that you want to sit neutral in the saddle. Your seat bones need to be pointing down, not sticking out the back or tucked too far under. It is the feeling in the seat that is ultimately important. So if your seat bones are not underneath you it will be very difficult to pick up on when the feet are moving.

Begin counting the feet out loud at first. If you are worried that other riders will hear you, say it softly so that only your horse knows you are counting. It is important to verbalize the count because this connects the left and right hemispheres of your brain. This is important when you have to "do" something corresponding to the count. Once you have mastered the exercises saying the count out loud you can switch to counting silently to yourself.

Start the canter from whatever gait is easiest for you. (Later we will discuss transitions from halt, walk, and trot.) Once in the canter begin to count out the rhythm. At first don't worry about which beat you started with. Just count "1, 2 ,3, 1, 2, 3" to yourself as you canter. Notice if simply counting the beats has already helped the horse to settle into a rhythm.

Then look for the moment of suspension. Count only this phase for a while by saying "up." Notice that as you focus on the suspension phase you become a bit lighter in the saddle. This will also allow the horse to lift a bit more through the back. Feel how the suspension goes all the way through out the top of your head. This is also true for the horse. The entire topline needs to be involved in creating the suspension from tail to poll.

Now look for the movement in the leading leg. If you are on the right lead, it will be the right front leg. If you are on the left lead, it will be the left front. Notice the landing/support phase of this leg. The horse's head will nod slightly downward as she comes over the leading leg in the support phase. Knowing when the leading leg is in support will be very important for timing the flying changes.

Next see if you can count the stride starting with the outside hind leg. It will be landing first after the moment of suspension. Finding the outside hind leg will be important for transitions into and out of canter. Then look for the feel of the landing phase of the diagonal pair of legs.

Finally put it all together again counting the three beats for each stride knowing which legs are on each beat that you count. Then simplify the count by only counting once for each full stride of canter. Notice that the three beats for each phase fit into one full count per stride. Then count the feet again within the stride. If you get the count right, the stride should remain the same regardless of how you are counting it (three counts/strides or one). The difference is that you can separate a full canter stride into its components and back again to a full stride.

Once you are able to feel and count the feet in canter you will be ready to correctly time transitions. You will take all the "guess work" out of the movements so that you can have smooth transitions every time.

Right lead canter	Rhythm count	Phase of stride	Photo
Left hind leg	"1"	landing	p. 130
Right hind/left front leg	"2"	landing	p. 131, top
Right front leg	"3"	landing	p, 131, bottom
	Moment of suspension all legs off the ground		

Left lead canter	Rhythm count	Phase of stride	
Right hind leg	"1"	landing	—
Left hind/right front leg	"2"	landing	—
Left front leg	"3"	landing	—
	Moment of suspension all legs off the ground		

Transitions into the Canter

T O MAKE SMOOTH TRANSITIONS INTO CANTER FROM HALT, WALK, AND trot the rider must know where the horse's balance is at the moment preceding the transition. If the horse is leaning on the forehand then the transitions will be rushed, heavy, and out of balance. However if the horse's weight is back on the hindquarters then the transitions will be light, easy, and smooth.

In order to adjust the balance the rider has to be able to shift the horse's weight onto the appropriate

Canter depart from the halt.

hind leg for the desired lead departure, then time the aids for the appropriate lead. More importantly the rider must remain in balance during the moment of the transition. Otherwise the horse will be knocked out of balance by the rider's weight shift.

Things that affect both the horse and rider in the transition are anticipation, breath holding, leaning forward, collapsing to one side, and stiffening the joints in the legs. It is important that the rider remain in the middle, in balance, receiving the movement of the horse in the legs yet firm in the torso so that the horse's change of gait is absorbed. If the rider stiffens her legs against the transition it will cause the horse to stiffen and result in a rushed, off-balance transition.

Conversely if the horse stiffens, anticipates the transition, holds his breath, etc., it can affect the rider. The rider will begin to prepare for the horse's reactions (rather than actions) which could potentially increase the resistance in the horse. The key is for the rider to be able to calmly prepare the horse for the transition without any reactive behaviors in either party.

Let's look at the balance needed to make a good canter depart. To strike off into right-lead canter the horse will have to coil over the left hind leg. For the left lead, the horse has to coil over the right hind leg (see photo on page 134). Coiling the hind leg (asking the horse to increase the angulation of the pelvis, hip, stifle, hock, and fetlock) by rocking back onto the hindquarters stabilizes the horse's overall balance. This allows the horse to lift the forehand into the transition. It is the same preparation you will need for down transitions from canter.

WEIGHT LIFTING

Think of a weight lifter about to press 500 pounds. In order to get underneath the load the weight lifter lowers his buttocks and coils his leg joints. He squats down towards the floor. This keeps his center of gravity low and over his feet and as close to the bar as possible. He has to be strong in his loins to stabilize his pelvis. He has to keep his center of gravity over his feet in order not to strain his back.

Then the weight lifter has to jerk the bar from the floor up to his chest and over his head. Once the bar is over his head he uncoils his legs and stands up. He has to hold the weight over his head long enough to demonstrate that he has the control, strength, and stability to support the weight.

If the weight lifter straightens up before the bar is overhead he will not be able to pick up the load. His center of gravity will be too high. In this case he may fall forward in the attempt and could potentially hurt himself. To be successful the weight lifter must first get underneath the load.

The horse demonstrates a similar weight-lifting mechanism. However, the horse is not just lifting vertically. The horse is also propelling horizontally. So the vector force is diagonal containing components of vertical lift and horizontal thrust. The amount of vertical vs. horizontal depends on the exercise. A more collected canter will have more lift whereas an extended canter will have more horizontal thrust.

The higher the degree of collection the lower the horse's pelvis must go. Also the greater the angulation required in the joints of the hind limb to lift the load. Remember that the weight lifter had to lower his center of gravity to get underneath the barbell by squatting. The horse must also get underneath his center of gravity before he can lift.

Since the horse is a quadruped (four-legged) its center of gravity is further forward in the body than the human (biped). The center of gravity in the horse is approximately at the 11th–12th ribs. Fortunately this is about where the rider is sitting when in a vertical position. Therefore, in order to lift himself and the rider off the forehand the horse needs

Sliding stop.

Levade

to lower the haunches and place the hind legs closer to his center of gravity.

A movement in a reining horse that requires an extremely high degree of collection is a sliding stop. Correctly executed the horse's pelvis is very low to the ground. The joints of the hind legs are flexed (coiled) with the hind feet deep underneath the body. The front end of the horse remains elevated with the back round. The front legs keep moving because the collection of the hindquarters allows the front end to remain free.

A classical dressage movement, the levade, also requires the horse's pelvis to be lowered close to the ground with the hind legs coiled. Levade is a preparatory move for airs above the ground. The front legs are tucked up in a position similar to when a horse jumps.

For the degree of collection required in a sliding stop or levade, the horse has to be very strong like a weight lifter. He has to lower his pelvis closer to the ground. He must be very well muscled in his loins to stabilize the pelvis. Finally he has to coil and stabilize his joints to keep his hind feet underneath his center of gravity (approximately where the rider is sitting). Then he can easily lift his front end and the rider up.

CANTER TRANSITIONS

In a good canter transition, the horse performs a hint of the movement similar to a sliding stop or levade. The horse has to slightly lower his pelvis and coil his hind legs to stabilize the body for the change of gait (see bottom photo, page 137). The amount of coiling and weight shifting depends upon the degree of collection and whether the departure is from halt, walk, or trot. In an upward transition the horse coils the hind legs then thrusts off into the new gait. In a down transition the horse coils and absorbs the movement to remain on the hindquarters and change gaits. (The bottom photo on page 137 could also represent the moment before a down transition to trot.)

"ALMOST CANTER" TRANSITIONS

Trot/canter transitions require the horse to support over his outside hind leg and slightly separate the diagonal pair of legs prior to the departure. In the forward trot the horse is equally balanced between the diagonal pair of legs. The horse's weight is evenly distributed throughout. The front and hind pairs of legs form even triangles.

In the preparation for the canter departure there is a slight shift of weight onto the outside hind leg while the horse continues to trot (see top photo at right). This creates a separation of the diagonal pair—outside hind/inside foreleg—necessary for the canter lead.

In most instances it is the last few strides of trot before canter when things go astray. In anticipation of the canter the rider holds his breath, tenses up, and tips forward out of balance. Instead of the horse balancing over the hindquarters, the weight shifts to the forehand creating a rushed transition. Practicing the weight shift to the hind leg just prior to the departure will prepare the rider for the canter transition without actually cantering. This also allows the horse to become comfortable with making the canter transition from the hindquarters rather than falling onto the forehand. Both the rider and the horse can learn how to remain in balance, breathing, and relaxed so that the transition itself is effortless.

To ride "almost canter" transitions you need to start with a good forward trot. If your trot is not forward enough then the horse will want to break to walk when you ask for the "almost canter." Next you want to time your aids as the outside hind leg is landing so that the hind leg coils (top photo). If you wait until the support phase it is too late because the leg is already thrusting (opening the joints).

From the rising trot you can ask for the "almost canter" at the top of the rising phase (if you are on the correct diagonal). This is the moment when the outside hind leg is landing. Think of being a bit slow at the top of the rise like trying to move through cold molasses or as if there is a bit of drag on your waist at the top of the rise. Direct your breathing towards your back and over the horse's hindquarters at that moment. You will feel the horse slightly delay in the trot stride.

Blondie and I are in trot. The triangle formed by her hind legs is slightly smaller than her front legs because I have prepared for the canter transition. The diagonal pair—outside hind/inside front—are just landing. This is the moment I ask Blondie to balance. Notice that I have remained vertical in my body position. I am letting the outside of my hip sink back in to the socket so that Blondie supports herself on the outside hind leg.

The moment of strike off into right-lead canter. Blondie is now responding by supporting herself on the outside hind leg. The departure is immediate, light, and in balance. Notice that she has lifted up through her withers and back into the canter. Also notice the leg sequence. The outside hind leg, after having coiled is still on the ground. The inside hind/outside front legs have pushed off the ground and remain united as a diagonal pair which initiates the canter stride. Compare this photo to the one above and see how the outside hind leg/inside front leg are now in a different pattern. Instead of moving together like a parallelogram (trot) they now form a "v" indicating that they are no longer diagonally united.

Blondie has good reach with the inside hind leg meaning this is a good forward walk. The outside hind leg is just ending its support phase. I have already coiled and balanced Blondie on the landing phase of the outside hind leg. I am now cueing her for the canter. Next the inside hind leg/outside front leg will push off the ground while underneath her center of gravity. This push provides the weight lifting upward thrust into the canter depart. The lead leg (inside front) is in flight phase.

Blondie has begun the canter. The diagonal pair of legs has already left the ground and she is beginning support phase of the leading leg. The outside hind leg is in flight coming underneath the body for the next canter stride.

Halt/canter transitions require the same weight-shifting balance as the previous trot/canter and walk/canter transitions. Blondie needs to rock her weight back onto the outside hind leg for support. The inside hind leg pushed off for the canter transition. If the weight comes down onto the inside hind leg the horse will fall forward and rush the transition rather than lift up. Therefore the inside hind leg provides the upward thrust for the transition.

If you are sitting the trot you still want to look for the landing phase of the outside hind leg. Breathe into your back in order to shift the horse toward the hindquarters.

At first you might need to close your fingers on the reins as you ask with your seat. This will help the horse understand that you want a weight shift to the hindquarters. As the horse begins to understand your seat aids you will need your hands less and less.

Once you feel the horse shift the balance back onto the outside hind leg release your aids and ride the trot forward and even again. Do this exercise several times until you feel the horse come back and go forward at the trot easily without needing your reins.

When shifting his weight onto the outside hind leg it is important to maintain your postural alignment (top photo, page 137). You are not creating this shift by leaning back or tilting your weight to the outside. Instead you create this shift by expanding your back which lets your pelvis tip under just a fraction. If you lean or tilt you will make it more difficult to use your back. The horse will stick in the hips instead of sink back into his hips.

TROT/CANTER TRANSITIONS

When the "almost canter" becomes easy, without anxiety on either part, then you can ask for the actual canter transition. If your preparation was good and your aids are clear the horse will easily pick up the canter. Even if you don't get the canter on your first attempt you will be able to support the horse by immediately returning to the "almost canter." Set up for the next canter depart and ask again.

To canter, start by asking for the "almost canter." If you feel the horse respond easily, simply add your canter aids without changing anything else. Remember to keep yourself balanced during the departure so the horse makes the transition from the hindquarters as in the bottom photo on page 137.

My aids for the canter depart are the "almost canter" to shift the horse's weight. Then I sink slightly into my outside hip. I follow this with the engagement of my inside seat bone (tightening the underside of my right buttock) to the get the inside hind leg to come under for the right lead. If necessary my outside leg reinforces the inside seat bone. It is really important that I remain vertical throughout the transition to keep the horse from falling onto the forehand. I lengthen up from my feet through the top of my head as the horse is striking off to canter. This helps me stay vertical and allows the horse to come up through the back (bottom photo, page 137).

It might help if you think of the outside seat bone as "can" (support) while the inside seat bone is "ter" (go). Therefore, I ride "can" "ter." If my horse fails to respond to my seat I can reinforce the aids with my outside leg. If she tries to rush off I catch her forward motion with my back ("almost canter") and the reins, sink into my seat ("can") and ask again on the next stride ("ter"). It is really important at that moment to remain in good alignment so that the horse is not also dealing with the rider's loss of balance. You might practice the depart on a hard chair with your hands underneath your seat bones so you can feel what you are doing before practicing on the horse.

WALK/CANTER AND HALT/CANTER TRANSITIONS

Walk/canter transitions require the same coiling mechanism as trot/canter transitions. You need a good walk with the "almost canter" feeling again occurring as the outside hind leg lands. It will actually feel like the horse "almost halts." This provides the horse with the outside hind leg for support into the transition. My canter aids are the same.

Blondie and I remain quiet in the halt. I prepare for the transition to canter by sinking my weight back through my outside hip, then I lengthen up through my body to the top of my head. She prepares by coiling her outside hind leg. If I had leaned back it would have caused her to stiffen in her outside hind leg instead of coil. Therefore I remain vertical yet sink back through my hip joint so that she will do the same thing. As I lengthen up Blondie increases her muscle tone so that she can lift her back into the transition.

In this canter departure, the diagonal pair of legs has pushed off into canter. The outside hind leg continues to remain in support of the overall balance. The lead leg, inside fore, is in breakover. Notice that Blondie has lowered her pelvis for the departure. Also notice that she is lifting up through her back and neck. I have remained in a vertical position so that she can stay over her hindquarters throughout the transition. Lengthening up through my spine stabilized my position and asked Blondie to lengthen through her topline. I asked for the transition by engaging my pelvis on the inside. To do this I activate my buttocks and hamstring muscles on the right, directing them towards her inside ear. My outside leg is ready to reinforce the request if she were not listening to my seat.

PART FOUR

LENGTHENING

Rigid Strength vs. Unbendable Strength

*I*N SEVERAL EXERCISES, I HAVE REFERRED TO "LENGTHENING." I THOUGHT it was about time I gave you a good explanation of what I meant by that term.

Lengthening refers to a way of using your muscle system to stabilize your body. Instead of seeking strength by shortening the muscles you can find strength in lengthening the muscles.

Lengthening muscles allows you to be strong without becoming rigid. It is how you can accomplish the illusive goal of

never pulling back on the reins when applying your aids. Your contact becomes solid yet giving vs. hard and pulling which happens when you use rigid strength. In order to understand how this works we need to understand a bit of anatomy.

YOUR ANATOMY

The skeleton is the framework for the body. It is comprised of bones. Without bones we would be like a jellyfish, a fluid-filled sack of organs slithering around on the ground. Therefore the bones provide support, protection for the organs, and structure allowing us to stand upright.

The place where bones meet each other are called joints. Joints give us flexibility. If we had only a few joints we would be more like stick figures or Barbie® dolls. This would make it really difficult to ride. We would not have the ability to conform to the horse's shape through our legs or absorb the

motion of the horse. The more angles you form in your legs the more movement you can absorb. (Hence the reason for riding with shorter stirrups for jumping and running cross-country.)

The joints provide us with a wide range of movements. Simply by combining the possibilities of several joints at one time we can do all sorts of things. It is said that we are born with over 7,000 different possible movements based on the number of bones and joints within our skeleton. However, by the time we leave high school we typically utilize only about 800 of these movements.

What creates or inhibits the movement of the bones? In part, the muscle system is responsible. Ligaments hold bones together like thick rubber bands. Tendons attach muscles to the bones. Muscles provide the contracting power that moves the bones. Combined with the nervous system (nerves, spinal cord, and brain), the neuromuscular system is responsible for coordinating our movement. If there is a muscle misfire you might wind up with a cramp. Conversely, if the muscle is not getting any neural input it

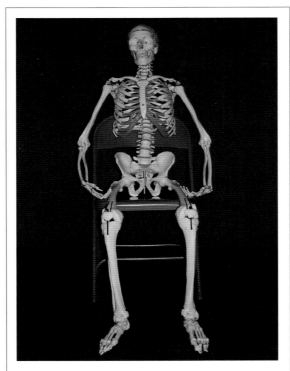

You are made up of a bunch of bones.

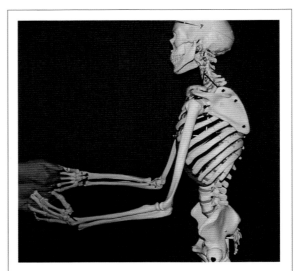

Joints allow you to bend and absorb motion, for example your elbow joints bend when holding the reins.

might not fire at all as seen when muscles atrophy because of nerve damage.

The nervous system is like the conductor of an orchestra directing and blending the different instruments (muscles). When you are functioning well the nervous system causes the muscles to fire at the right moment to create an organized movement just like the sound of a professional orchestra. When things aren't as coordinated, the movement is more like the sound of your local elementary school band.

COORDINATION

Coordination is one of the major differences between a really good rider and an average rider. Similar to the elementary school kid that has not sufficiently practiced his instrument, many young riders haven't had enough practice time. However, adult riders may not have used the specific coordination required for riding when they were young so they don't have access to those motor patterns. Injuries and childbearing also play a role in the loss of neuromuscular patterns. Therefore adult riders have to find ways to develop the coordination they've lost or never had.

When learning a new movement (or a new song) or remembering an old one the neuromuscular system goes through a process of trial and error until the desired result has been achieved. It is best to allow for that learning process in both horses and humans rather than create tension by demanding immediate results.

Tension inhibits the neuromuscular system's ability to learn the new movement. In fact, muscle tension is one of the greatest inhibitors of good performance. Simply remember what happened the last time someone yelled at you while you were trying to do something new with your horse to know what that feels like. Even if you wanted to do what the trainer asked, having that

pressure on you made it much harder if not impossible because you tensed up. Yet muscle tone is absolutely required to ride well.

There is a huge difference between tension and tone. Have you ever shaken hands with someone who squeezed your hand so hard it hurt? That's like the rider who uses too much muscle to ride. The horse feels squeezed. Tone is sufficient muscle tension for the action without excess. This would be shaking hands with someone who has a firm but gentle handshake or the good relaxed rider who only uses what is needed to get the job done. When a muscle is flaccid there is insufficient muscle tone. This is the "limp wrist" version of a handshake. It is equivalent to the rider who sits like a sack of potatoes.

When we are well toned, the muscle can provide the right amount of effort. Then when the nervous system supplies the impulse, the muscles contract at the right time to coordinate the movement. So how do the muscles move bones?

CREATING MOVEMENT

Some of the muscles responsible for moving your limbs work in pairs. By having pairs of muscles we have the ability to flex joints (close the angle between the bones) or extend them (open the angle between the bones). Examples of muscles working in pairs are the biceps/triceps on the front and back of your upper arm and the quadriceps/hamstrings on the front and back of your thigh. When you extend your knee the quadriceps muscles are contracting. When you bend your knee the hamstrings are contracting.

Also, it is important to note that muscles only work in contraction. When you bend your arm at the elbow, the biceps (the Popeye the Sailor Man muscle) is contracting while the triceps (that flabby underarm muscle) is relaxed. When you do a push-up the triceps are working while the biceps are sitting idle.

If both muscle groups contract at the same time the joints become rigid. Rigid joints make your body like a stick figure. Joints can be locked without the person appearing to be overly tense. That's because internal muscles can be holding the joint rigid while external muscles are at rest. The result of having a locked joint can make the person tense because they are unable to do a specific movement involving that area. The joint that needs to function can't so the rest of you has to try to make up for it.

A classic example of compensation is someone with rigid ankles. When a rider has rigid ankles they have to find some other way to stay on the horse because this important shock absorbing joint is not working. Riders with rigid ankles often wind up gripping with their knees and thighs, arching or rounding their backs, and hanging onto the reins for support.

When one joint in your body becomes rigid other joints automatically follow suit. Even your breathing will become restricted. Essentially the joints become gridlocked like a traffic jam in a major city—all of the intersections become blocked by cars and no one can go anywhere even when the lights turn green. To get out of rider grid-lock muscles need to let go. Then movement can occur.

To feel how stiffening one joint can effect others do the following exercise. Shake one hand in the air. Now tighten one finger and shake your hand again. Notice what happened to your hand, the other fingers, your wrist, and your breathing. They have all become stiff. It is really difficult to remain "soft" on the horse's mouth if even one joint in your hand becomes rigid.

Sometimes joints get rigid when we perform a specific movement (e.g., the exercise above) because the neuromuscular system contracts too many muscles at once. Other times the joints are locked even when we think we are not asking for any movement at all. This could be due to a variety of causes—injuries, shortened ligaments, habits, etc. When the joint is locked even at rest there is little chance of it moving properly when we ask it to move. This is why people go to chiropractors—to get the joints functioning properly again.

To feel what it is like to have a locked joint versus a properly functioning joint do the following exercise. Take your left index finger and gently press back on the tip of your relaxed right index finger. Notice that there is spring in the knuckle joint (where the finger joins the palm). The springy response means you are feeling the muscle/tendon/ligament system rather than feeling a restriction in the joint. Next make your right index finger rigid. Press on it again. Feel how the spring in the knuckle joint is gone. Now it feels like a rigid object. Any movement you feel is limited to the tip of your finger, not at your knuckle because you have locked the knuckle joint.

RIGID VS. UNBENDABLE STRENGTH

The rigid rider who tenses and locks her joints is unable to absorb the motion of the horse. This type of rigid strength is brittle and limited. When this strength fails it can result in injury because the weakest part of the system will go first. This weak point might not be the muscles but instead the bones, tendons, or ligaments. Or the rider may lose her balance.

Think of the last time you saw someone being dragged around or yanked out of the saddle by her horse. The rider became even more anxious and tried harder to stop the horse. Yet all she succeeded in doing was making it easier for the horse to pull her around because she became more rigid. Pretty soon the rigid person's strength will run out—the muscles fatigue and the rider will let go or collapse.

When muscles are in a constant state of contraction (rigid strength) they are not getting enough oxygen to run efficiently. The by-product of this inefficiency (called anaerobic metabolism) is lactic acid. As the lactic acid levels rise the muscles reach a point where they can no longer contract, so they stop. The muscles will feel extremely weak at that point.

The build up of lactic acid is the cause of soreness in the muscles. It takes time for the circulatory system (bloodstream) to clear out the lactic acid from the muscle. This is one of the reasons that body builders don't work the same muscle group every day. The muscles need time to recover from intense exertion and strengthen to handle another workout.

In teaching riding the practice of working a rider to fatigue is often used to create a change in their position. The instructor will push the student through the incorrect pattern thereby exhausting the gripping muscles so that they finally quit working. Then the rider suddenly discovers another group of muscles that can keep her from falling off. The down side to this is that this approach is incredibly stressful on both the horse and the rider. It can take a while for the muscles to fatigue and in the meantime the horse is being pounded in the back. Not to mention that most adults ride for pleasure and don't enjoy being subjected to such methods.

Training horses to the point of exhaustion is also a method used by some trainers. The horses are worked until their muscles fatigue at which point they "cooperate." The down side to this technique is that the chances of tendon and joint injury are vastly increased. As the muscles fatigue they can no longer support the joints properly, which creates wear in the joints. The workload is then placed on the ligaments and tendons. If the muscles are not rested long

enough after such an exertion they are more easily damaged. In addition the incorrect muscles are strengthened so that it takes longer and longer to get the horse "soft" and "cooperate."

The coordinated rider only uses the right amount of muscle to resist the forces of the horse and apply the aids. Therefore his muscles are able to relax "catch their breath," and continue to recharge before the next effort. The circulatory system is able to supply the muscles with oxygen so that they don't have to use the anaerobic method, which produces lactic acid. Instead the muscles are able to maintain aerobic metabolism; in other words, they use oxygen which helps make muscle fuel. The rider is much less likely to fatigue or have overly sore muscles afterward.

In order to be strong while remaining in motion, the muscles have to dampen the movement of the joints without locking. Therefore only the muscles necessary to inhibit the movement act while the rest of the muscles remain at rest. This unbendable strength comes from lengthening the muscles rather than shortening them.

Overall strength has little to do with unbendable strength or the size of the person. It has everything to do with how you use what you have. I have seen a ten-pound dog dragging his owner around on the leash because the owner was rigid. I have also seen little children able to withstand horses' strength when they use their unbendable strength.

Here is an exercise to learn how to use unbendable strength vs. rigid strength. This exercise is commonly called the Unbendable Arm. It is a Martial Arts technique. You can apply this concept in all different ways like Unstraightenable Arm, Unbendable Leg, or wherever you need to be soft yet strong.

In doing the Unbendable Arm exercise you will need someone to help you. There

Kristen is attempting to bend my arm while I am holding it rigid. I have locked my knees, tensed and raised my shoulder, and come forward with my upper body. My fist is clenched and I am looking down at Kristen. Notice the amount of tension in my face. My breathing is restricted. While Kristen might not be strong enough to bend my elbow she could easily pull me forward off my feet at this moment without very much effort because my entire body is braced.

I am now using my Unbendable Arm strength to resist Kristen. Notice that my hips, knees, and ankles are soft and grounded. My pelvis is under me in a neutral position and my head is balanced over my feet. I am breathing easily, my elbow is slightly bent, and my hand open. I am looking ahead of me. Kristen has applied pressure to my elbow in an attempt to bend it. Since she is unable to do that she is also pulling on my arm. As Kristen pulls I sink into the joints in my legs and "ground" myself so that she cannot pull me off balance. She also tried pushing. Again I sank down into my joints and directed my energy forward out my arm.

are a few rules that are important to avoid injury. Make sure the person testing your arm places one hand flatly down onto the elbow joint and has the other hand on your forearm just before your wrist (see photo above left). Make sure that your elbow bends down toward the ground as your forearm comes up and back to you. Also make sure your palm is facing sideways or toward the sky (see photos above). This way you will avoid the possibility of injuring the elbow joint.

Now make your arm straight and rigid. Have your helper attempt to bend your arm. If she is unable to bend it, have her push or pull on your arm and see if she can knock you off balance. Notice how much effort you have to use to resist the person attempting to bend your arm. Also notice what happens to your breathing. (See above photo, left.)

Next, let your arm hang down. Separate your feet so that they are about hip width apart. Have one foot in front of the other. Check to make sure your pelvis is in neutral with your seat bones pointing straight down. Breathe into your back and allow the person to lift your arm without helping. Notice how difficult it is to not use any muscle when they lift your arm! Have her let go of your arm and just let it simply hang in space. Leave a slight bend in the elbow with your fingers softly extended. This keeps your joints from locking. Make the decision that your arm is going to stay straight and look out ahead of you.

Have the assistant test your arm again. Remember the purpose of the exercise is to give you the feeling of strength using Unbendable Arm, not whether or not your helper is stronger than you. So if the person testing your arm feels it start to weaken have them maintain that amount of pressure. Check that your hips, knees, and ankles are slightly bent. Think of sitting slightly to soften your hip joints. Again make the decision that your arm will stay straight. Think of sending a blast of water up from your feet out your hands toward a distant object. You will need to keep pulsing energy out your fingers and "sitting" as the person applies more pressure to avoid becoming rigid.

When your arm is unbendable you might notice that it doesn't feel like you are doing much of anything to resist your assistant. You will be able to wiggle your fingers and breathe easily. You might have the feeling of putting your arm gently through the sleeve of your shirt as you lengthen your arm away. Notice how little effort this takes on your part.

When you are unbendable the assistant should be able to push and pull on you without loss of balance. As she pushes you, absorb the force by sinking into to your back leg joints and sending more energy forward out your arm. When she pulls you, sink into your front leg and feel like you are holding her with your back. This way you can resist both pushing and pulling without leaving your middle position. (See photo on page 146, right.) This is also the feeling for the "almost" rebalancing for transitions.

28

Applying "Unbendable Strength" to Riding

FTER THE LAST LESSON THAT INTRODUCED THE DIFFERENCE between rigid strength (stiffening joints and shortening muscles) and unbendable strength (keeping joints flexible and lengthening muscles), we'll look at how this concept applies to riding. When you ride with unbendable strength, you can support yourself within the movement of the horse without bracing and eliminate the resistance caused by rigid strength.

Hopefully you were successful in doing the Unbendable Arm

exercise from the last chapter. Could you feel the difference between the Unbendable Arm vs. the Rigid Arm? When tested, you could easily be pushed or pulled out of balance when you were rigid. But with unbendable strength your balance was a lot harder to disturb.

When tested, did you notice that the effort required to sustain the unbendable arm was far less than that needed when using rigid strength? You were able to breathe even though someone was pushing hard on your arm, whereas with rigid strength, your breathing was shallow and restricted. Unbendable strength will greatly decrease fatigue and allow you to use fine motor control when riding. Therefore, unbendable strength requires less effort and allows you to refine your aids.

Did you also notice what it felt like to test the other person's arm? Perhaps you felt the hardness of the rigid strength vs. the elastic quality of the unbendable strength. When testing the rigid strength did you also become rigid and try really hard? Maybe you noticed that there was less desire to keep testing the unbendable strength. You could feel that the other person's arm wasn't going anywhere, so why bother? This reaction is similar to how the horse responds when you use unbendable strength vs. rigid strength when riding.

As an example of the reaction to rigid strength, remember when you were a kid and someone shoved you around. You got mad and shoved back. Pretty soon the two of you "locked horns" as both were steadily pushing on each other waiting for the other person to give in. You became rigid and stiff, digging your heels into the dirt. Part of this shoving response is due to how the nervous system responds to pushing and bracing.

When you push or pull on someone that is braced the response from your nervous system comes from the brain stem. In other words the message that the nervous system receives goes from your hand up the brain stem at the base of your skull and cycles back to your hand. The message doesn't get to the thinking portion of your brain. The response is essentially a reflex reaction. Therefore, pulling or grabbing at the reins is not a conscious decision. You have to overcome the reaction and get to the thinking part of your brain. Changing your reaction is a lot easier when your reflex to grab is not activated first. This reaction will also change more quickly if you have another option.

When you are "unbendable" you bypass the reflex reaction and get to the thinking part of the brain. Hence you can analyze what you are feeling. There is more opportunity to respond to the input rather than react. In fact you may never even enter a reflexive-pulling phase because with unbendable strength you are lengthening the muscle, or giving, not pulling.

You can't prevent the reflex response if you are rigid or out of balance. However you can train yourself to respond differently as long as you seek balance first in response to the pull. By consciously practicing how to override this reaction, seeking balance first and then responding to what you felt, you can train yourself out of the habit of pulling completely.

Here is an exercise to demonstrate the reflexive nature of pulling. Take hold of your helper's hand. Stiffen your legs and lean back similar to a braced horse. Without saying anything notice how your helper responds. Almost invariably the other person will lean back immediately to stop you from falling. In a few cases he might move forward a step or two but if you keep leaning he will "catch" you. Rarely will the other person not pull back. Ask your helper to lean back against you so you can do this exercise. (Notice that if he did not lean back he remained in balance and kept stepping into your pull most likely because he has already trained himself out of the reflexive reaction.)

Your partner leaned back because he felt you falling. His unconscious automatic reaction was to catch you. If you continue to lean once he has caught you, he has little choice but to brace back. The two of you wind up in a dependent balance. If either one of you were to let go the other person would fall down. Notice that if you try to move around it is stiff and awkward. Both of you will move with short and choppy steps because you are not in a position where you can move freely. Your joints are rigid rendering certain movements impossible.

To get out of the dependent balance one of you is going to have to change what you are doing. Decide between you who is going to be the "rider" for this next part. If you like, have the "horse" close his eyes. Then, as the "rider," bring yourself into good alignment with your head over your feet. Bend your hips and knees slightly. What did your partner do? Did he change his stance? Lean out of balance again and see what happens. Notice that you stiffened your hips and knees when you leaned out of balance. Repeat this several times making the amount of change less and less. Watch your partner and see how he responds to your shifts of balance. While remaining in good alignment move around and see how easily your partner moves with you. Then lean slightly out of balance and notice what happens.

The moment the rider alters her balance by leaning, the partner will automatically counter-balance the move. This will occur even with a very slight shift of weight. When you are in the dependent balance it is very hard to move because so much effort is required just to keep standing. Both parties are rigid in their legs and arms so there is

little joint flexibility left for movement. When the "rider" goes into a neutral alignment the ability for both parties to move increases dramatically. This is because their joints are no longer rigid.

When the rider moves into a neutral position (independent balance) she no longer needs her partner. If her partner continues to pull, the rider has choices. One choice is that she can let go, allowing her partner to fall on the floor (i.e., throw the reins away). Another is to give one arm forward a little to encourage the other person to rebalance (release of one rein). A third choice is to assist the other person in finding her balance by maintaining contact with the hand while using your body in a way that corresponds to your partner's body. This will give the partner the specific information of how to bring herself into balance. In other words, if the partner is not using her hip joints the rider can squat down. This will encourage the partner to use her hips thus bringing her into more independent balance.

The rider has these options because she is no longer balancing against her partner. She can bypass the reflexive reaction and take positive action to rebalance the horse, who is falling on the forehand. In the neutral position the rider can influence the horse through the seat, legs, and reins to assist the horse in finding his own balance (self-carriage). In this way the rider can overcome the brace in the horse and show him how to move using his own body. However, if the rider is unable to remain in neutral, is pulled out of balance even slightly, the horse/rider pair will start to brace against each other again.

That's one of the reasons why learning the "unbendable strength" technique is so important. If you can balance yourself and act thereby breaking the cycle of pulling, the horse will stop pulling back. If the horse is seriously habituated to pulling you can stop yourself from "buying in" to the behavior. You can respond through your "use of self" to remain in balance. Then correct the problem through application of your aids. Unbendable strength gives you the physical support you and the horse need to sustain independent balance while the horse is learning a new pattern.

When you make yourself rigid you are set up to pull. Period. In fact that set-up occurs the moment your body is no longer aligned with your seat bones underneath you. Remember that the seat bones provide you with a base of support. When we have no base of support (pelvis and legs) your brain automatically finds some way to keep you from falling. If the reins are handy, that's what you use. Some people have learned to ride like this quite elegantly. However they have had to override the resulting retraction of the arm (pull) so that they still give towards the horse's mouth. This means they had to use a second muscle action to prevent the first. If they had their pelvis underneath them in the first place they would have eliminated the resistance right from the beginning. In addition they would be able to access the unbendable strength to give forward to the horse automatically.

A pull is different from a hold. You can hold the other person's hand or the rein without pulling. This is more like holding a child's hand while walking the child across the street vs. dragging the child out of the candy aisle at the grocery store. You can maintain the same amount of pressure in your hand but alter the feeling by how you use the rest of your body. It can shift from uncomfortable to pleasant depending on how the rest of your body is functioning.

Go back to the above exercise where you leaned back. Repeat the exercise maintaining a moderate pressure in your hand grip. Go from the leaning position into correct

body alignment. What happened to the feeling in your hand vs. the feeling in the overall balance? Lean back again. Try to "fix" the other person's position with your hand without bringing yourself into balance. Notice that he looks unhappy because all you are doing is jerking him around. Now bring yourself into balance without altering your grip. Notice that your partner came into balance. Also notice that the feeling in the grip changes. It becomes part of the overall feeling not just a hard hand squeeze. Now you are holding instead of pulling because you are in balance. Your partner will feel the contact shift from his hand (horse's mouth) to an even feeling connected to your body.

Next think of using your unbendable arm and internally lengthen your arm towards the other person. How did he respond? Did he soften his arm and shoulder as you

Kristen has allowed her back to round while I am pulling on her. Rounding her back has brought her seat bones too far under. This makes it impossible for Kristen to access her unbendable strength. Instead she has stiffened her arms and gone up on her toes. She is pushing off the ground and pulling through her back and arms to resist me. Notice that her elbows have straightened and become rigid. Observe how I have also tucked my pelvis under also and stiffened my right leg thereby bracing back against her. If either one of us were to let go we would both fall down.

Again Kristen is unable to access her unbendable arm strength in this arched posture. She is leaning back, pushing off her toes, and stiffening her arms to resist me. Notice that I have also leaned back against her. We are holding each other up in a dependent balance. If either of us were to let go now we would both fall backwards. She cannot give the reins away without falling.

Here Kristen is sitting deeply with her seat bones pointing straight down. Her feet are flat on the ground. She has a base of support between her pelvis and feet. She is able to maintain a bend in her elbow while I pull because she is using her unbendable strength to resist me. Notice how her entire body is involved in this position as the work is shared throughout the entire system. In contrast, notice that in the previous two photos your eye is drawn to specific parts of Kristen's body whereas in this photo you see it as a whole.

Kristen now would be able to give the reins by letting go, moving her arm forward slightly, or lengthening her arm in order to give me a release.

lengthened? Pull your arm back slightly and tense your muscles. What was the reaction now? Most likely he tensed as well.

When you use unbendable strength not only do you quit pulling—you start giving. You give the other person or the horse a place to go. You suggest that they no longer have to brace or stiffen because you are no longer dependent on them for your balance. Suddenly the other person or horse starts to move more freely. Notice that when you did the above exercise you felt comfortable rather than restricted, guided rather than told.

Remember that unbendable strength is a concept. It does not mean that your elbow is always held in the same position. Instead

think of it as a way of being strong regardless of what position you are in. It does require that you be in a good balance to access this type of strength. Lengthening the muscles will provide the support to maintain whatever position you choose without making the joints rigid.

The photos in this chapter demonstrate the same concept in a sitting position vs. standing. The same principles apply. Being on the ball is more closely related to sitting on the horse.

29

Lengthening Up Through Your Spine

CHAPTER 27 FEATURED THE ANATOMY OF MOVEMENT AND AN EXERCISE called the Unbendable Arm. Unbendable strength differs from stiff strength in that the joints remain movable rather than rigid and is achieved by lengthening muscles rather than shortening them.

In Chapter 28, we discussed the idea of independent vs. dependent balance. If the rider is in a dependent balance (rigid, leaning, or tilting) then the unbendable strength cannot be accessed because the rider is

> I can't push this student over when she lengthens.

braced against the effects of gravity. In order to access the unbendable strength the rider must first balance over her feet in alignment with gravity. Balancing over the feet frees the joints and allows the muscles to support the joints rather than locking them in order to be strong.

In addition we found that there is a difference between a "holding" (or supporting) rein vs. a "pulling" rein. A supporting rein implies that the reins are not needed for the rider's balance because the rider is balanced over her feet. A pulling rein means that the rider does not have a base of support (pelvis in neutral, legs underneath the seat). Therefore the rider is using the reins for balance. When unbendable strength is applied to a supporting rein it is actually a giving contact because the rider is lengthening the muscles in the arm. The horse can feel this lengthening just as you would if you did the exercise with the partner described in the last chapter.

In this chapter, we will look at how you can apply the concept of lengthening to the core of your body. When you lengthen through the spine you can begin to create collection in the horse by allowing the horse's back to come up underneath your seat. In order for the horse to collect he must lengthen through his topline (poll to tail). This is the equivalent of the rider lengthening through her spine.

Collection is achieved when the horse lengthens the back and lowers the haunches which then elevates the head and neck and flexes the poll. If however, the horse's head is set without lengthening through the topline the horse is not collected. This false frame is commonly seen and often confused with true collection.

In false collection the horse is shortening the back rather than lengthening the back. Instead of a round look the horse will be concave along the topline. Shortening the

back will create problems such as sore backs, front-end lameness, hock damage, and high-headedness not to mention the countless training problems seen that are ultimately due to back pain. If you have ever had a pain in your back I am sure you can relate to what it must feel like to a horse with a sore back carrying two or three hundred pounds of human and saddle.

CONCENTRIC VS. ECCENTRIC MUSCLE WORK

So how exactly is lengthening the muscle different from shortening it? Lengthening your muscles is called "eccentric" contraction. Shortening your muscles is "concentric" contraction. When the horse uses his body correctly he lengthens his topline — eccentric contraction. If the horse shortens the back muscles—concentric contraction—then the topline shortens, the back drops, his hindquarters go out behind, and his head goes up.

As an example of eccentric vs. concentric contraction do the following exercise. Pick up something heavy like a bucket full of water and lift it with your elbow by your side (like a curl in weight lifting). This is concentric contraction of the biceps. The triceps is relaxed. Now very slowly lower the object down. This is eccentric contraction of the biceps. The triceps remains in relaxation. Now do a push-up off the floor. This is concentric contraction of the triceps; the biceps is in relaxation. Very slowly lower yourself back down to the floor. This is eccentric contraction of the triceps.

To understand how lengthening your back is stronger than shortening, do the following exercise. Find someone to help you. Be careful not to injure each other. It would be best to pick someone who does not have any back problems for this exercise. A teenager would be a good choice.

Have your partner pretend to be a horse by getting down onto the floor on "all fours" (knees and palms). Use a carpeted surface or something soft to protect her knees. Now place your thumbs into her back just behind the shoulder blades a couple of inches away from the spine. Press in with your thumbs. Most likely your "horse" just dropped her back down towards the floor. The back muscles have shortened. Notice what happened to the pelvis. Most likely it tipped up and out, behind the person. Also notice that the head and neck raised up. The topline is now shortened. In order to get the head down you might get the horse to yield in the poll but the neck will still be shortened and there will be a large bulge in the underneck muscles.

Notice that you cannot put very much weight onto the "horse's" back in this position without dropping her to the ground.

Now place your hands on the sides of the "horse's" rib cage and give the ribs a lifting hug. Notice that the "horse" lifts the back up. Observe how the clothing on your "horse's" back has changes from lots of wrinkles (when the back was down) to stretching the fabric when the back comes up. Place your palms onto the "horse's" back and press down. Notice how much weight you can apply without any sign of weakness. In most cases I can put almost my entire body weight onto the "horse's" back when it is up vs. almost no weight when it

Kristin is slumping on the ball. In this posture she is unable to lengthen upward through the back. Her head is in front of her seat. Therefore she is not in postural alignment. The front of her body is contracted. The back muscles are relaxed and unable to stabilize her position. If I pushed on her now I would easily push her forward off the ball. Note that her feet have rolled to the outside so that she would be unable to lengthen down through her legs to keep from being pushed over.

Kristen has placed herself in postural alignment. Her seat bones are underneath her. Her abdomen and back are stabilizing the torso. The back is flat at the waist. There is a straight line from her ear through her shoulder and hip. Kristin's feet are flat on the ground so that she can lengthen down through her legs. When I apply a force to her waist she is able to stabilize her body with minimal effort. Notice that although she is sitting up straight she does not look stiff. Her shoulders are relaxed. In order to have her hands in "rider position" she would only have to bend her elbows to lift her hands.

is down. The back is now lengthening. Notice that as the back came up the pelvis dropped down and forward and came underneath the torso. The "horse" engaged her hindquarters.

So how does the rider get the horse to lengthen through the back while under saddle? The rider must be able to lengthen through his own back to encourage the horse to do the same. The difference is that the rider lengthens in a vertical direction while the horse lengthens horizontally since horses are on all fours.

HOW A PERSON LENGTHENS THROUGH THE BACK

If you are in poor skeletal alignment (feet out in front, head poking forward, or seat bones out behind you) you will be unable to lengthen properly. So the technique of lengthening requires good alignment.

In fact you can use the concept of lengthening to find good alignment of your body.

I have moved up Kristen's back and am now applying a force to the area between her shoulder blades. As I move up my hand Kristen must continue to lengthen through her back from her head to her seat. If she concentrated on the area where I applied the force she would round her upper back and I would push her over. Instead she has remained lengthened throughout the entire back and can therefore resist me with a minimum of effort. Notice that her rib cage is expanded at the front which has raised her sternum from underneath. Pulling her sternum up would cause Kristen to arch her back and make it easy for me to push her over. Again notice that her back appears flat. The natural curves of the spine remain. However the muscles have filled in the curves by lengthening so that the back appears flat. If Kristen contracted the back muscles you would see an arch in her back.

I am now testing whether Kristen has lengthened through her neck by applying a light pressure at the back of her head. If Kristen had not lengthened through the neck I would easily be able to push her head forward. Notice that if Kristen takes the force I am exerting on her head and sends it down and up through her spine. In other words she does not try to "push" back with her head and neck against me. Instead she received the push and distributes it throughout her spine therefore allowing her to remain stable. If she were to push against me at this point she would be the equivalent of the horse bracing upward against the bit.

As you begin the process of feeling yourself lengthen you will notice if your head is forward, your ankles restricted or your pelvis tipped. You will need to change these things as you go in order to lengthen all the way through your spine.

Remember that this is the same thing as the Unbendable Arm exercise we did previously. Only now we are applying that concept through the body. The sensation of lengthening is an expansion from the inside of your body. You might feel like you are growing out the top of your head. Or you might think of a good stretch when you first wake up in the morning.

Lengthening is not simply pulling or pushing your head up. When you lengthen

I am now pushing directly down on Kristen's head. She is lengthening upward and therefore feels extremely stable. She is gently pressing upwards against my fingers. Essentially Kristen has aligned and lengthened her spine to resist any forces exerted either forward, backward, downward or upward. In other words, she has stabilized her spine using her postural muscles by lengthening the muscles.

it is as if you have more space inside of you in all directions. Your joints might feel like they have a bit more room in which to move. Just as your arm felt like it was growing away from you in Chapter 27 and your legs met the ground in Chapter 28 you will now notice an overall sense of growing down toward the ground, expanding front and back and up out the top of your head.

It might be useful to think of walking with a book on the top of your head like they did in the old days to develop good posture. Imagine having something balanced on the top of your head and finding a way to keep it balanced there as you move around by growing tall to meet it. If you go too far you will arch your back. If you don't grow enough you will be slumping. Lengthening is the middle ground.

An arched back posture would be similar to the position in the above exercise with the person on all fours and the back down. In an arched back position the back muscles are shortened.

APPLYING LENGTHENING WHILE MOUNTED

When mounted, as you lengthen upward through the top of your head you draw your body in a vertical direction. Think of sucking a thick milkshake up through a straw. You create a vacuum or lift through your seat which draws the horse's back up into your seat. However, you don't want to hold this as hard as you can for the rest of your life. You do want to be able to pulse this lifting feeling upward in order to ask the horse to lift his back up into your seat. As he does that you can gently relax and feel how his back has risen. Notice that your legs will close slightly around the horse when you lengthen up. Some people think of this feeling as giving the horse a hug with their legs. You want the hug to start from the lower leg upward into the seat rather than pinching down from the thigh. Down from the thigh will drop your lower leg off the horse and may cause him to drop the back rather than lift it.

Notice what muscles you use when you lengthen and "hug" your horse with your legs. You may feel a bit of tension in the lower part of your buttocks. This is OK. You will feel it where your thigh and your buttocks meet. For women who deal with "saddle bag" thighs, this will definitely help toward reducing the bags!

You may also notice that it feels like your seat bones lift a little bit off the saddle. Again this is because you are engaging your "hindquarters" just as you want the horse to do.

When the horse lifts the back up into your seat he is lengthening the back and abdomen. If he overly contracts the abdominal muscles

he will go "behind the bit." If he overly contracts the back he will go "above the bit." In both cases he will lose the forward/upward thrust from the hindquarters and fall onto the forehand. When he lengthens both the underline and topline he will lift the mid-section of his body, stabilize it, and therefore be able to push off the ground from a hind foot placed well underneath the body to lift upward.

For those of you interested in learning more about lengthening check out the Alexander Technique, a method developed by F.M. Alexander in the late 1800s that works to change movement habits in every-day activities, teaching students to maintain alignment and lengthen rather than shorten themselves as they move. There are books available and Alexander Technique practitioners throughout the world.

30

Why Is Lengthening the Back So Important?

LENGTHENING THE BACK CREATES STABILITY THROUGH THE SPINE. IN order to elevate the forehand the horse has to lift and stabilize the midsection of his body. When the midsection is stabilized the horse can drive forward from behind. The pelvis tilts underneath which helps the hind legs reach deeply underneath the body. When the hind legs push from deep under the body they create a forward/upward thrust. Take a look at my horse Andy on the next page.

Suspension is created in the trot when the horse lengthens through the spine.

Andy is lengthening through his topline and underline.

Notice that his back is lifted. The right side of the pelvis has come down and forward as the right hind leg swings deeply under his body. This leg is providing support while the outside hind leg is thrusting him forward. Look at the elevation in the front end. Notice that the withers are up and the neck is lengthening out of the shoulders. Also observe how the abdominal area is engaged to support the midsection. Andy has lengthened through his entire topline from his poll to his tail. This creates an "uphill" canter with lots of energy.

If the back drops the pelvis will tip out and back (arched back posture). The driving force of the horse will occur after the body of the horse has already passed over the hind leg ("push-back engagement"). The resulting force is forward and down driving the horse on the forehand. The back muscles will be shortening rather than lengthening. The horse cannot lift the rider and the forehand up. The rider's weight will additionally push the back down unless the rider overrides this action and lengthen upwards.

In motion the lift in the horse's back is not created by contraction of the abdominal and back muscles. Instead the gait creates the movement which is "caught" and dampened by the abdominal and back muscles so that the torso becomes more stable. In other words, the back muscles limit the upward oscillation and the abdominal muscles limit the downward oscillation of the torso. Hence lengthening the muscles catches the movement rather than creating it. This is also why the walk is the hardest gait to correct once the horse has dropped his back.

In walk there is no suspension to create any upward oscillation of the torso. Once the horse has dropped the back in the walk it will take a lot of good training to correct. A "pacey" walk commonly results when the horse has a contracted topline. The rider has to encourage the horse to lengthen through the spine to lift the back. In order to do that the rider must first lengthen her back.

Trot has some suspension and therefore increases the amount of oscillation in the torso. If the horse's back is up you will have a round trot, which is easy to sit. But if the horse has dropped and the back muscles have shortened the trot will be choppy and hard to sit. By asking for a strong forward (not fast) movement in trot the back will begin to stay up.

The very nature of canter creates vertical lift of the torso and therefore is the best gait for the horse to naturally lengthen the back. However, if something impedes this motion then the canter will be severely affected. Saddles that don't fit, poor rider position, sore muscles and/or foot problems can all contribute to cantering with the back shortened rather than lengthened.

Again look at Andy's photo. Notice the firm abdominal line. This phase of the stride (about to land the diagonal pair of legs) is when the greatest downward force is exerted on the midsection. It is now that the muscles must lengthen to catch the torso. If the back shortens at this point the torso will sink further shortening the neck and tipping the pelvis out and back.

31

The Deep Seat

Y OU HAVE HEARD HORSEMEN TALK ABOUT THE DEEP SEAT. "TAKE A

deep seat and a faraway look," is a common statement with

cutting horse trainers. "Sit down!" can be heard across dres-

sage arenas. "Sit deep on the

approach," is a typical instruction

in jumping.

Classic examples of riders with

a deep seat are Ray Hunt, one of

the founders of the current clinic

scene; Arthur Kottas-Heldenberg,

Chief Rider at the Spanish Riding

School in Vienna, Austria; Bill

Steinkraus, Olympic gold medal stadium jumper; and the late Nuno Oliveira, the Portuguese classical dressage Master. Therefore, as a rider you know sitting deep is something you should aspire to in your riding.

In addition to deepening the entire seat, there are times when you are told to put more weight on one side of your seat than the other. Some trainers tell you to put your weight on the inside or outside seat bone, depending on the exercise you are doing. Weighting one seat bone can be the cue for canter departures, bending, and lateral work.

Most riders lean over to one side or push down onto one stirrup to weight one seat bone. However, these methods can actually cause the seat bone to lift up. As the seat bone rises, the rider's seat lightens instead of deepens.

In this final chapter on lengthening, we will look at how to put your weight down onto the seat bones, thereby deepening the seat. By placing one or both seat bones down, you can create more stability. This will become an important concept as you apply these techniques later on. First, however, consider what makes your seat deep.

PUSHING, TILTING, AND LEANING

What happens to your seat when you try the two most common tactics (pushing with foot and tilting or leaning) to sit deep? Notice what your seat bone does and whether you have retained or lost mobility in your legs during the following exercises. Sit on a hard surface. If you happen to have a saddle on a strong saddle stand that you can sit on safely, that would work too. Place one hand underneath your seat bone on that same side (i.e., left hand, left seat bone). Later, repeat the exercise with your other seat bone and hand.

Push your whole foot against the floor or stirrup on the same side as your hand. Does your seat move up off the chair (saddle) or down? Can you move your leg anymore? Does it make a difference if you push your toes or your heel to the floor? By pushing down to deepen your seat, you can actually push your seat out of the saddle.

Notice that when you push your foot against the floor, your buttocks and thigh muscles tighten. If you only push your heel down, the back of the leg tightens. If you push your toe down the front of the leg tightens. Regardless of how you push your foot to the floor, you wind up stiffening all the joints in your legs so you lose flexibility. You will not be able to use your leg correctly to time your aids with the motions of the horse.

Next, lean over that hand that is under your seat bone. Whether you collapse your rib cage or tilt your torso will determine the results you feel.

If you collapse your rib cage, observe that the pelvis tilts up on that side and therefore lifts the seat bone off the chair. If you lean over, you might feel your seat bone crush your fingers. Notice that the seat bone presses toward the center of the chair when you tilt. When you are in the saddle, this sends pressure toward the horse's spine instead of down onto his back.

Compare what happens to your legs with both tilting and collapsing. Observe that it becomes very difficult to lift one of your feet off the floor. In both cases, you are out of balance. Therefore, you cannot pick up both feet at the same time. That means you can't use your legs independently from your seat when riding. It will take a lot of effort to use your legs at all if you collapse or tilt to weight your seat because your legs will be busy holding you on.

Finally, observe that your seat bone didn't really go down—it went sideways toward the center of the chair and up. You didn't actually deepen your seat at all! You moved your whole body to try to deepen your seat. Instead of making your seat more effective, independent, and subtle, it became dependent, restricted, and hard.

In this experiment you attempted to deepen one seat bone at a time. It would be impossible to deepen both seat bones at the same time through leaning or collapsing. When you lean, the opposite seat bone lifts; you totally lose one of your seat bones. When you collapse, you lift the seat bone you want to lower; again, you don't have both sides.

Pushing on both feet in an attempt to deepen the seat pushes you up and out of the saddle. Have you ever seen riders sit way up on the cantle of their saddle when they have their feet or heels jammed down? They are pushing their seat out. They have to use a lot more grip and shoulder strength to remain in the saddle, which will only cause more tension in the horse. In order to deepen their seat, they will need to do a lot less muscle work.

LETTING YOUR SEAT BONES DOWN

So how can you deepen your seat on one side or the other without causing all these other things to happen? The answer is by relaxing the muscles around the hip joints and then lengthening through the back.

Kristen is sitting heavily on her seat, but she is not sitting deep. If I pushed down on her head at this moment, I would be able to shorten her overall height and push her off the ball. Her pelvis is rolled under. The "ASIS" is behind her pubic arch (rounded back).

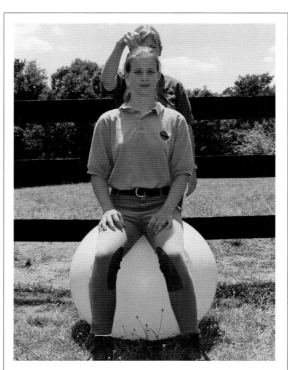

Kristen's pelvis is in a neutral position. Her right seat bone sinks down onto the ball and she lengthens upward through her right side. I place my fingers on the right side of her head and press gently to give her a place to lengthen into. The distance from the top of her pelvis to her armpit is longer on the right side than the left. I can press down firmly on her head without disturbing her position. In fact, Kristen is extremely strong right now.

Recall the exercise with your hand under one seat bone. Sit on your hand again with your fingertips on your seat bone. Check that your pelvis is in a neutral position (seat bone pointing straight down).

To check that your pelvis is in neutral, place your hand on your waist with your fingers cuffing your side, thumb toward your back. Slide your hand down until it rests on the bony prominence of your pelvis. The top of your pelvis is known as the iliac crest. Follow this ridge with your thumb toward the front of your body and down toward your leg. You will come to a point that sticks forward. Its name is the Anterior Superior Iliac Spine (ASIS).

Next, locate the top of your pubic arch. This is the edge closest to your belly button. With one hand on the ASIS and the other on your pubic arch, line the two up so that they are on the same plane across the front of your pelvis as if both would touch a wall in front of you. Your seat bones should be pointing down, with your pelvis in neutral. If the ASIS is behind your pubic arch, you are rounding your back. If the ASIS is in front of the pubic arch, you are arching your back (there will be some slight variation on this based on each individual's conformation).

Return your hand underneath your seat bone. With a neutral pelvis, tighten the muscles around your seat bone and feel it lift up off your hand. Now completely relax the muscles so that you only feel the seat bone on your fingers. Tighten and release until you can easily feel the seat bone in your fingers or only the muscles in your fingers. The range of muscle tone required for riding varies with the activity. In a canter departure, I engage that muscle on the lead-leg side seat bone. For a rein back, I relax that muscle a bit.

Notice that when you relax the muscles around your seat bone, you stop pushing your foot against the floor. Instead, your foot will rest on the floor (or the stirrup). Your leg will hang rather than grip. Your seat bone sinks into your hand when you stop pushing on your foot.

Next, put your hand on your thigh. Push your foot into the floor. Observe that when you push, especially a bit more on your toe, your quadriceps muscles (topside of your thigh) tighten. When you stop pushing they let go. If you push a bit more on your heel, the hamstrings (underside muscles) tighten.

Follow the quadriceps muscle up toward the crease of your jeans formed by the bend of your hip joint. You will feel some cord-like tendons there. These are the attachments in the quadriceps. Feel how tight they get when you push on your foot? See if you

Kristen is repeating the exercise on the left side. Her left seat bone sinks down into the ball as she lengthens up through her body into my hand. Kristen puts more weight on her left seat bone without altering her overall position.

can get them to feel like there is some slack in the cord. You will have to quit pushing on your foot.

Repeat the loosening of your quads and hamstrings with your hand under your seat bone. What happens to the seat bone? Can you feel your seat bone get deeper? As the quads stop contracting, the seat bone can sink into your hand or the saddle. Also, notice that when you stop pushing, the crease in your jeans gets a little deeper as the ball of the hip joint sinks back into the hip socket.

Experiment with the tension of the muscles around your hip joint, buttocks, quadriceps, and hamstring muscles. Notice that when you relax these muscles your seat bone deepens and your hip relaxes without altering the position of your pelvis.

Kristen deepens both seat bones and lengthens through both sides of her body. Her legs hang down and meet the ground while she grows taller. She is very stable in this position. I push firmly on her head and can't disturb her posture. She has deepened her seat effectively.

However, simply relaxing the musculature of the hip and pelvis is not enough to create a deep seat.

The problem is that you need muscles to stabilized your body while you relax in the seat. If you are unable to stabilize your spine, you will wind up pushing, gripping, and tightening the seat all over again as soon as the horse moves.

LENGTHENING THROUGH THE SPINE

This is where lengthening comes in. By lengthening up through your spine, you create the support and stability necessary to leave the seat bones down in the saddle. In fact, lengthening will deepen the seat bones further. Then you can apply a seat aid, contract the muscles around the seat as necessary, and relax them again after you have applied your aid. This allows you to have the same kind of refinement in your seat as you would in your hands or legs. You can pick your horse up through your seat or sit into him, depending on how you tone the seat muscles.

To feel the effect lengthening has on your seat, place your hand underneath one seat bone. Feel the seat bone in your fingers and relax the musculature around it. Now think of lengthening up through your spine over the seat bone as you did in Chapter 29. Imagine that there is a line running from your seat bone vertically through your body and alongside your ear. Notice how that side of your body lengthened upward while at the same time your seat bone dropped into your hand.

Repeat this same exercise on the other side. You are now able to effortlessly deepen your seat and place more weight over one side of your seat without disturbing your overall balance.

Deepen both seat bones at the same time. Think of your seat bone melting down into your hands. Relax the musculature around the hip joint. At the same time imagine that someone has put a book on the top of your head. You are now lengthening over both seat bones. Feel what happens to your breathing. Notice that it feels like you have some room to breathe. There is more space between your seat and your head. This will afford your horse room to expand as well.

The ability to deepen your seat by lengthening will help you maintain your overall balance throughout your ride. You can practice this while driving your car, sitting through a meeting, or talking to someone during dinner. By practicing in all kinds of environments, you will be ready when your horse decides to make a sudden move. Instead of gripping yourself out of the saddle, you will be able to sink effortlessly.

Conclusion

SOMETHING THAT IS ELEGANT IS GENERALLY SIMPLE—A SLINKY BLACK dress, a crisp button-down white shirt and blue jeans. This elegance is due to the lack of something rather than the addition of others. It is the same with riding a horse.

It is not the addition of aids but the reduction of aids that makes riding appear effortless and smooth; horse and rider in harmony. Further, it is the reduction of excess movement that results in the clarity of your aids. The horse can hear what you are asking much better when you are in

balance and therefore able to ask clearly. Hopefully after going through these lessons you have discovered for yourself the simplicity of each movement.

The secret to the timing of the aids is your ability to apply them independently and at the appropriate moment. This can only happen once you have achieved the balance of your own body, the understanding of the aid's effect and when to apply them. But once achieved the grace by which both horse and rider can move will be enhanced just like the lines of good classic clothing enhance the wearer.

It takes a lot of patience to work through some of these lessons. Stick with it; you will be pleased with the results. Your horse will be more responsive and willing because you are asking for movements at the moment that he can comply rather than when he can't. If you get stuck, go back to the previous chapter and start again.

Sometimes you might find yourself confused. A great way to resolve confusion is to get down on all fours and crawl around. Feel where your weight is and what you have to do to execute the movement yourself. By thinking and experimenting you not

only will understand the lessons in this book, you will understand how to work out other ideas on your own.

Always take it back to the simple concept of gravity and balance. Look at a skeleton, both horse and human. This is the framework we have to deal with in gravity. When the force is going through the bones the muscles won't have to stiffen. Movement becomes more fluid. If the skeleton is not in balance then the muscles have to work a lot harder to keep us (or the horse) from falling first. This can cause a mental (lack of understanding) and emotional (fear) imbalance as well as a physical (pain) imbalance.

If what you are doing isn't giving you the desired result, change something. It will only make it better or worse. If worse, then you know that's not the direction you want to go. If better, figure out what you did and why it worked.

Ask questions of yourself, your teachers, and your friends. Don't simply accept my or anyone else's opinion as the ultimate authority. Many times I have thought something was one way only to discover that there was another option. Had I not been willing to listen to my student's "dumb" questions I might never have discovered another possibility.

When your get off your horse and you are scratching your head, be glad. It means you are about to learn something. The bad days are almost more important than the good ones because they cause us to question, reflect, puzzle over a problem, and wonder what went wrong. It is in these moments that we often learn the most. It may have been a hard day for your horse but ultimately he will thank you because you are going to have a different solution to the problem tomorrow.

Horses are willing to forgive us when they know we are trying. They also feel when we get it right because carrying us becomes effortless and they are able to comply with our request—something they seem always willing to do when we listen to them.

I hope that after reading this book you begin to question, think, and discover something about yourself. I hope you think about your riding in a different light. It is the awareness of yourself and how you move with your horse that will ultimately produce the partnership you seek. Have fun with these ideas. Adapt them to your purposes and allow yourself to enjoy your successes.

About the Author

*W*ENDY MURDOCH GREW UP IN STAMFORD, Connecticut, and has spent her entire life involved with horses. She has ridden since childhood and competed in and been interested in a variety of disciplines, from hunters to dressage, eventing and reining. Wendy holds a B.S. in Animal Science from the University of New Hampshire and an M.S. in Equine Reproductive Physiology from the University of Kentucky. She is constantly expanding her education. Her credentials include being a TT.E.A.M. Practitioner II/Clinician and a Senior Level IV Centered Riding® Instructor. She is currently studying to become a Feldenkrais Method® Practitioner, the concepts of which she already integrates into her clinics. In addition Wendy studies with holistic veterinarian, saddle-fitting expert, and author Dr. Joyce Harman and Bettina Drummond, the only authorized representative of the Nuno Oliveira School from Portugal.

In her clinics over the past 17 years, Wendy has taught riders of all disciplines and skill levels how to use their bodies to achieve a higher level of performance with their horses. Some of her students have never been on a horse before while others compete at the highest levels of their discipline. Her goal is to make riding fundamentally simple by showing riders how to achieve what great riders do naturally. Her clinics are held year round in the United States, Canada, and Europe and have included Africa, Australia, and New Zealand.

Visit her website at www.wendymurdoch.com for a clinic schedule and for more information about The Murdoch Method. Contact her at info@wendymurdoch.com for a copy of her brochure or a catalog or call her office at 866-200-9312.

Index

Carriage House Publishing

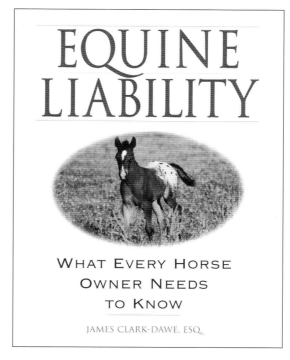